P9-DHZ-325

March of America Facsimile Series

Number 84

History of the Donner Party

Charles Fayette McGlashan

History of
the Donner Party
by Charles Fayette McGlashan

ANN ARBOR

UNIVERSITY MICROFILMS, INC.

A Subsidiary of Xerox Corporation

56708

Foreword

Even before the discovery of gold in California, stories of the opportunities in that land of sunshine and flowers had reached the East, and emigrants were beginning to move across the plains and mountains in a trickle that would soon reach the proportions of a flood. In the summer of 1846, a group known as the Donner Party left Independence, Missouri, headed for California. Their tragic denouement, marooned in the snows of the High Sierras, where they spent the winter, reduced to starvation and ultimately to cannibalism, was described in numerous contemporary newspaper stories. The story of the Donner Party, reported by survivors and their rescuers, created a sensation. Many versions were soon in circulation in this country and in Europe, some of them contradictory and many of them highly sensational. Finally C. F. McGlashan attempted to sort out the true from the false and to present a rational account of what had really happened. The result was his *History of the Donner Party: A Tragedy of the Sierras*, first printed in 1879 at Truckee, California. The book was immediately popular. A seventh edition had appeared by 1902. In 1940 the Stanford University Press published an annotated edition with a bibliography, prepared by George H. Hinkle and Bliss McGlashan Hinkle.

McGlashan's *History of the Donner Party* has been one of the principal sources for later retellings of this grim story. The author interviewed survivors, tried to reconcile contradictory statements, looked up diaries and journals kept by members of the party, sought out contemporary newspaper reports, and presented as clear an account as was possible. Despite old-fashioned verbiage and sentimental and pious ruminations by the author, McGlashan's narrative is vivid and convincing.

The Donner Party proper numbered ninety people when it left Independence, then the principal staging area for emigrants headed west. Other groups joined the party until a train numbering between two and three hundred wagons stretched for two miles along the trail. Later, says McGlashan, survivors asserted that "certain imposters and falsifiers claim to have been members of the Donner Party, and as such have written untruthful and exaggerated accounts of the sufferings of the party."

The Donner Party moved across the Great Plains, on past Salt Lake, with the usual quarrels and dissensions that marked such expeditions. Bickerings about routes and the order of travel caused some delays and they did not reach the mountains until after the middle of October. Already Indians had driven off many of their oxen and horses and the party was forced to abandon their wagons and walk. Their supplies were also reduced to bare subsistence levels. To make matters worse, snow began to fall and constant storms, earlier than usual, soon made passage over the mountains impossible. Scattered in the region east of what is now known as Donner Pass, the miserable emigrants made such shelters as they could and prepared to spend the winter where they were. Before their ordeal was over, many had died and some had reached that stage of desperation that made them feed on the flesh of the dead. Forty-eight survived, according to McGlashan, and at the time of his writing "twenty-six, possibly twenty-eight" were still living.

A modern account of this episode is that by George R. Stewart, *Ordeal by Hunger: The Story of the Donner Party* (New York, 1936). See also Bernard DeVoto, *The Year of Decision, 1846* (Boston, 1943).

HISTORY

OF THE

DONNER PARTY.

A Tragedy of the Sierras

BY C. F. McGLASHAN.

PUBLISHED BY

CROWLEY & McGLASHAN,

(Proprietors Truckee Republican,)

TRUCKEE, CAL.

PRESS OF H. S. CROCKER & CO.,
Sacramento.

FRANK FOSTER, BINDER,
Sacramento.

PREFACE.

—— ——

THE delirium preceding death by starvation, is full of strange phantasies. Visions of plenty, of comfort, of elegance flit ever before the fast-dimming eyes. The final twilight of death is a brief semi-consciousness in which the dying one frequently repeats his weird dreams. Half rising from his snowy couch, pointing upward, one of the death-stricken at Donner Lake may have said, with tremulous voice: "Look! there, just above us, is a beautiful house. It is of costliest walnut, inlaid with laurel and ebony, and is resplendent with burnished silver. Magnificent in all its apartments, it is furnished like a palace. It is rich with costly cushions, elegant tapestries, dazzling mirrors; its floor is covered with Oriental carpets, its ceiling with artistic frescoings; downy cushions invite the weary to repose. It is filled with people who are chatting, laughing and singing, joyous and care-free. There is an abundance of warmth and rare viands, and sparkling wines. Suspended among the storm-clouds, it is flying along the face of the precipice at a marvelous speed. Flying? no! it has wheels and is gliding along on a smooth steel pathway. It is sheltered from the wind and snow by large beams and huge posts which are bolted to the cliffs with heavy iron rods. The avalanches, with their burden of earth and rocks, and crushed pines, sweep harmlessly above this beautiful house and its happy inmates. It is drawn by neither oxen nor horses, but by a fiery, hot-breathed monster, with iron limbs and thews of steel. The mountain trembles beneath his tread, and the rocks for miles re-echo his roar."

If such a vision was related, it but indicates, prophetically, the progress of a few years. California's history is replete with tragic, startling events. These events are the landmarks by which its advancement is traced. One of the most mournful of these, is recorded in this work—a work intended as a contribution, not to the literature, but to the history of the State. More thrilling than romance, more terrible than fiction, the sufferings of the Donner Party form a bold contrast to the joys of pleasure seekers who to-day look down upon the lake from the windows of silver palace cars.

The scenes of horror and despair which transpired in the snowy Sierras in the Winter of 1846–7, need no exaggeration, no embellishment. From all the works heretofore published, from over one thousand letters received from the survivors, from ample manuscript, and from personal interviews with the most important actors in the tragedy, the facts have been carefully compiled. Neither time, pains· nor expense have been spared in ferreting out the truth. New and fragmentary versions of the sad story have appeared almost every year since the unfortunate occurrence. To forever supplant these distorted and fabulous reports—which have usually been sensational newspaper articles—the survivors have deemed it wise to contribute the truth. The truth is sufficiently terrible.

Where conflicting accounts of particular scenes or occurrences have been contributed, every effort has been made to render them harmonious and reconcilable. With justice, with impartiality and with strict adherence to what appeared truthful and reliable, the book has been written. It is an honest effort toward 'the truth, and as such is given to the world.

C. F. McGLASHAN.

TRUCKEE, CAL., June 30th, 1879

CHAPTER I.

HREE miles from Truckee lies one of the fairest and most
picturesque lakes in all the Sierras. Above, and on either
side, are lofty mountains, with castellated granite crests,
while below, at the mouth of the lake, a grassy, meadowy
valley widens out and extends almost to Truckee. The
body of water is three miles long, one and a half miles
wide, and four hundred and eighty-three feet in depth.

Tourists and picnic parties annually flock to its shores, and Bier-
stadt has made it the subject of one of his finest, grandest paintings.
In Summer, its willowy thickets, its groves of tamarack and forests
of pine, are the favorite haunts and nesting places of the quail and
grouse. Beautiful, speckled mountain trout plentifully abound in
its crystalline waters. A rippling breeze usually wimples and dimples
its laughing surface, but in calmer moods it reflects, as in a polished
mirror, the lofty overhanging mountains, with every stately pine,
bounding rivulet, blossoming shrub, waving fern, and—high above
all, on the right—the clinging, thread-like line of the snow sheds of
the Central Pacific. When the railroad was being constructed,
three thousand people dwelt on its shores; the surrounding forests
resounded with the music of axes and saws, and the terrific blasts

exploded in the lofty o'ershadowing cliffs, filled the canyons with reverberating thunders, and hurled huge bowlders high in the air over the lake's quivering bosom.

In Winter it is almost as popular a pleasure resort as during the Summer. The jingling of sleighbells and the shouts and laughter of skating parties can be heard almost constantly. The lake forms the grandest skating park on the Pacific Coast.

Yet this same Donner Lake was the scene of one of the most thrilling, heart-rending tragedies ever recorded in California history. Interwoven with the very name of the lake are memories of a tale of destitution, loneliness and despair which borders on the incredible. It is a tale that has been repeated in many a miner's cabin, by many a hunter's camp-fire, and in many a frontiersman's home, and everywhere it has been listened to with bated breath.

The pioneers of a new country are deserving of a niche in the country's history. The pioneers who became martyrs to the cause of the development of an almost unknown land deserve to have a place in the hearts of its inhabitants. The far famed Donner Party were, in a peculiar sense, pioneer martyrs of California. Before the discovery of gold, before the highway across the continent was fairly marked out, while untold dangers lurked by the wayside and unnumbered foes awaited the emigrants, the Donner Party started for California. None but the brave and venturesome, none but the energetic and courageous, could undertake such a journey. In 1846 comparatively few had dared attempt to cross the almost unexplored plains which lay between the Mississippi and the fair young land called California. Hence it is that a certain grandeur, a certain heroism seems to cling about the men and women composing this party, even from the day they began their perilous journey across the plains. California, with her golden harvests, her beautiful homes, her dazzling wealth and her marvelous commercial facilities, may well enshrine the memory of these noble hearted pioneers, pathfinders, martyrs.

The States along the Mississippi were but sparsely settled in 1846, yet the fame of the fruitfulness, the healthfulness and the almost tropical beauty of the land bordering the Pacific, tempted the members of the Donner Party to leave their homes. These homes were situated in Illinois, Iowa, Tennessee, Missouri and Ohio. Families from each of these States joined the train and participated in its terrible fate; yet the party proper was organized in Sangamon County, Illinois, by George and Jacob Donner and James F. Reed. Early in April, 1846, the party set out from Springfield, Illinois, and by the first week in May had reached Independence, Missouri. Here the party was increased by additional members, and the train comprised about one hundred persons.

Independence was on the frontier in those days, and every care was taken to have ample provisions laid in and all necessary preparations made for the long journey. Ay, it was a long journey for many in the party ! Great as was the enthusiasm and eagerness with which these noble-hearted pioneers caught up the cry of the times, "Ho ! for California !" it is doubtful if presentiments of the fate to be encountered were not occasionally entertained. The road was difficult, and in places almost unbroken ; warlike Indians guarded the way, and death in a thousand forms hovered about their march through the great wilderness.

In the party were aged fathers with their trusting families about them, mothers whose very lives were wrapped up in their children, men in the prime and vigor of manhood, maidens in all the sweetness and freshness of budding womanhood, children full of glee and mirthfulness, and babes nestling on maternal breasts. Lovers there were, to whom the journey was tinged with rainbow hues of joy and happiness, and strong, manly hearts whose constant support and encouragement was the memory of dear ones left behind in homeland. The cloud of gloom which finally settled down in a death-pall over their heads was not yet perceptible, though as we shall soon see, its mists began to collect almost at the outset, in the delays which marked the journey.

The wonderment which all experience in viewing the scenery along the line of the old emigrant road was peculiarly vivid to these people. Few descriptions had been given of the route, and all was novel and unexpected.   In later years the road was broadly and deeply marked, and good camping grounds were distinctly indicated. The bleaching bones of cattle that had perished, or the broken fragments of wagons or cast away articles, were thickly strewn on either side of the highway.   But in 1846 the way was through almost trackless valleys waving with grass, along rivers where few paths were visible save those made by the feet of buffaloes and antelope, and over mountains and plains where little more than the westward course of the sun guided the travelers.   Trading-posts were stationed at only a few widely distant points, and rarely did the party meet with any human beings save wandering bands of Indians.   Yet these first days are spoken of by all of the survivors as being crowned with peaceful enjoyment and pleasant anticipations.   There were beautiful flowers by the roadside, an abundance of game in the meadows and mountains, and at night there was singing, dancing and innocent plays.   Several musical instruments and many excellent voices were in the party, and the kindliest feeling and good-fellowship prevailed among the members.

The formation of the company known as the Donner Party was purely accidental.   The union of so many emigrants into one train was not occasioned by any preconcerted arrangement.   Many composing the Donner Party were not aware, at the outset, that such a tide of emigration was sweeping to California.   In many instances small parties would hear of the mammoth train just ahead of them or just behind them, and by hastening their pace, or halting for a few days, joined themselves to the party.   Many were with the train during a portion of the journey, but from some cause or other became parted from the Donner Company before reaching Donner Lake.   Soon after the train left Independence it contained between two and three hundred wagons, and when in motion was two miles in length.

With much bitterness and severity it is alleged by some of the survivors of the dreadful tragedy that certain impostors and falsifiers claim to have been members of the Donner Party, and as such have written untruthful and exaggerated accounts of the sufferings of the party. While this is unquestionably true, it is barely possible that some who assert membership found their claim upon the fact that during a portion of the journey they were really in the Donner Party. Bearing this in mind, there is less difficulty in reconciling the conflicting statements of different narrators.

The members of the party proper numbered ninety, and were as follows:

George Donner, Tamsen Donner (his wife), Elitha C. Donner, Leanna C. Donner, Frances E. Donner, Georgia A. Donner and Eliza P. Donner. The last three were children of George and Tamsen Donner; Elitha and Leanna were children of George Donner by a former wife.

Jacob Donner, Elizabeth Donner (his wife), Solomon Hook, William Hook, George Donner, Jr., Mary M. Donner, Isaac Donner, Lewis Donner and Samuel Donner. Jacob Donner was a brother of George; Solomon and William Hook were sons of Elizabeth Donner by a former husband.

James Frazier Reed, Margaret W. Reed (his wife), Virginia E. Reed, Martha F. (Patty) Reed, James F. Reed, Jr., Thomas K. Reed and Mrs. Sarah Keyes, the mother of Mrs. Reed.

The two Donner families and the Reeds were from Springfield, Illinois. From the same place were Baylis Williams and his half-sister Eliza Williams, John Denton, Milton Elliott, James Smith, Walter Herron and Noah James.

From Marshall County, Illinois, came Franklin Ward Graves, Elizabeth Graves (his wife), Mary A. Graves, William C. Graves, Eleanor Graves, Lovina Graves, Nancy Graves, Jonathan B. Graves, F. W. Graves, Jr., Elizabeth Graves, Jr., Jay Fosdick and Mrs. Sarah Fosdick (nee Graves). With this family came John Snyder.

From Keokuk, Lee County, Iowa, came Patrick Breen, Mrs. Margaret Breen, John Breen, Edward J. Breen, Patrick Breen, Jr., Simon P. Breen, James F. Breen, Peter Breen, and Isabella M. Breen. Patrick Dolan also came from Keokuk.

William H. Eddy, Mrs. Eleanor Eddy, James P. Eddy, and Margaret Eddy came from Belleville, Illinois.

From Tennessee came Mrs. Lavina Murphy, a widow, and her family, John Landrum Murphy, Mary M. Murphy, Lemuel B. Murphy, William G. Murphy, Simon P. Murphy, William M. Pike, Mrs. Harriet F. Pike (nee Murphy), Naomi L. Pike, and Catherine Pike. Another son-in-law of Mrs. Murphy, William M. Foster, with his wife, Mrs. Sarah A. C. Foster, and infant boy George Foster, came from St. Louis, Missouri.

William McCutchen, Mrs. W. McCutchen, and Harriet McCutchen, were from Ray County, Missouri.

Lewis Keseberg, Mrs. Phillipine Keseberg, Ada Keseberg, and L. Keseberg, Jr., Mr. and Mrs. Wolfinger, Joseph Rhinehart, Augustus Spitzer, and Charles Burger, came from Germany.

Samuel Shoemaker came from Springfield, Ohio, Charles T. Stanton from Chicago, Illinois, Mr. Halloran from St. Joseph, Missouri, Mr. Hardcoop from Antwerp in Belgium, Antoine from New Mexico, John Baptiste, a Spaniard, who joined the train near the Santa Fé trail, and Lewis and Salvador, two Indians, who were sent out from California by Captain Sutter.

The Breens joined the company at Independence, Missouri, and the Graves family overtook the train one hundred miles west of Fort Bridger. Each family, prior to its consolidation with the train, had its individual incidents. William Trimble, who was tráveling with the Graves family, was slain by the Pawnee Indians about fifty miles east of Scott's Bluff. Trimble left a wife and two or three children. The wife and some of her relatives were so disheartened by this sad bereavement, and by the fact that many of their cattle were stolen by the Indians, that they gave up the journey to California, and turned back to the homes whence they had started.

An amusing incident is related in the Healdsburg (Cal.), Flag, by Mr. W. C. Graves, of Calistoga, which occurred soon after his party left St. Joseph, Missouri. It was on the fourth night out, and Mr. Graves and four or five others were detailed to stand guard. The constant terror of the emigrants in those days was Indians. Both the Pawnees, the Sioux, and the Snakes were warlike and powerful, and were jealous, revengeful, and merciless toward the whites. That night a fire somehow started in the prairie grass about half a mile from camp. The west wind blowing fierce and strong, carried the flames in great surging gusts through the tall prairie grass. A resin weed grows in bunches in this part of the country, generally attaining the height of four or five feet. The night being very dark, these weeds could be seen standing between the fire and the guards. As the flames swayed past the weeds, the impression was very naturally produced upon' the mind of a timid beholder that the weeds were moving in the opposite direction. This optical illusion caused some of the guards to believe that the Indians had set fire to the grass, and were moving in immense numbers between them and the fire with intent to surround them, stampede the cattle and massacre the entire party. The watcher next to Mr. Graves discovered the enemy and rushed breathlessly to his comrade to impart the intelligence. Scarcely had Mr. Graves quieted him before it was evident that a general alarm had been spread in the camp. Two other guards had seen the Indians, and the aroused camp, armed to the teeth, marched out to give battle to the imaginary foe. It was a rich joke, and it was some time before those who were scared heard the last of the resin Indians.

Only once, before reaching Salt Lake, did death invade the joyous Donner Company. It was near the present site of Manhattan, Kansas, and Mrs. Sarah Keyes was the victim. This estimable lady was the mother of Mrs. J. F. Reed, and had reached her fourscore and ten years. Her aged frame and feeble health were not equal to the fatigues and exposures of the trip, and on the 30th of May they laid her tenderly to rest. She was buried in a coffin carefully fashioned from the trunk of a cottonwood tree, and on the brow of a beautiful knoll overlooking the valley. A grand old oak, still standing, guards the lonely grave of the dear old mother who was spared the sight of the misery in store for her loved ones. Could those who performed the last sad rites have caught a vision of the horrors awaiting the party, they would have known how good was the God who in mercy took her to Himself.

Chapter II.

THE following letters present an interesting glimpse of the first portion of the journey. They were written by Mrs. Tamsen Donner and were published in the Springfield (Illinois) Journal. Thanks for copies of these letters are due to Mrs. Eliza P. Houghton of San Jose, Mrs. Donner's youngest daughter. Allusions are made in these letters to botanical researches. Mrs. Donner, C. T. Stanton, and perhaps one or two others who were prominent actors in the later history, were particularly fond of botany. Mrs. Donner made valuable collections of rare flowers and plants. Her journal, and a full description of the contents of her botanical portfolios, were to have been published upon her arrival in California.

Though bearing the same date, the letters here presented were written at different times. The following appeared in the Springfield Journal, July 23d, 1846:

NEAR THE JUNCTIONS OF THE NORTH }
AND SOUTH PLATTE, June 16th, 1846. }

MY OLD FRIEND: We are now on the Platte, two hundred miles from Fort Laramie. Our journey so far has been pleasant, the roads have been good and food plentiful. The water for part of the way has been indifferent, but at no time have our cattle suffered for it. Wood is now very scarce, but "buffalo chips" are excellent; they kindle quick and retain heat surprisingly. We had this morning buffalo steaks broiled upon them, that had the same flavor they would have had upon hickory coals.

We feel no fear of Indians, our cattle graze quietly around our encampment unmolested.

Two or three men will go hunting twenty miles from camp; and last night two of our men laid out in the wilderness rather than ride their horses after a hard chase.

Indeed, if I do not experience something far worse than I have yet done, I shall say the trouble is all in getting started.   Our wagons have not needed much repair, and I cannot yet tell in what respects they could be improved.   Certain it is, they cannot be too strong. Our preparations for the journey might have been in some respects bettered.

Bread has been the principal article of food in our camp.   We laid in 150 pounds of flour and 75 pounds of meat for each individual, and I fear bread will be scarce.   Meat is abundant.   Rice and beans are good articles on the road; cornmeal too is acceptable. Linsey dresses are the most suitable for children.   Indeed, if I had one, it would be acceptable.   There is so cool a breeze at all times on the plains that the sun does not feel so hot as one would suppose.

We are now four hundred and fifty miles from Independence. Our route at first was rough, and through a timbered country, which appeared to be fertile.   After striking the prairie we found a first-rate road, and the only difficulty we have had has been in crossing the creeks.   In that, however, there has been no danger.

I never could have believed we could have traveled so far with so little difficulty.   The prairie between the Blue and the Platte rivers is beautiful beyond description.   Never have I seen so varied a country, so suitable for cultivation.   Everything was new and pleasing; the Indians frequently come to see us, and the chiefs of a tribe breakfasted at our tent this morning.   All are so friendly that I cannot help feeling sympathy and friendship for them.   But on one sheet what can I say?

Since we have been on the Platte we have had the river on one side and the ever varying mounds on the other, and have traveled through the bottom lands from one to two miles wide with little or no timber.   The soil is sandy, and last year on account of the dry season the emigrants found grass here scarce.   Our cattle are in good order, and when proper care has been taken none have been lost.   Our milch cows have been of great service, indeed.   They have been of more advantage than our meat.   We have plenty of butter and milk.

We are commanded by Captain Russell, an amiablè man.   George Donner is himself yet.   He crows in the morning and shouts out "Chain up boys—chain up," with as much authority as though he was "something in particular."   John Denton is still with us.   We find him useful in the camp.   Hiram Miller and Noah James are in good health and doing well.   We have of the best people in our company, and some, too, that are not so good.

Buffaloes show themselves frequently.

We have found the wild tulip, the primrose, the lupine, the eardrop, the larkspur, and creeping hollyhock, and a beautiful flower resembling the bloom of the beech tree, but in bunches as large as a small sugar-loaf, and of every variety of shade, to red and green.

I botanize, and read some, but cook "heaps" more.   There are four hundred and twenty wagons, as far as we have heard, on the road between here and Oregon and California.

Give our love to all inquiring friends.   God bless them.   Yours, truly,

MRS. GEORGE DONNER.

The following letter was published in the Journal of July 30, 1846:

SOUTH FORK OF THE NEBRASKA, ⎞
10 MILES FROM THE CROSSING, ⎬
TUESDAY, June 16th, 1846. ⎠

DEAR FRIEND: To-day at nooning there passed, going to the States, seven men from Oregon, who went out last year.   One of them was well acquainted with Messrs. Ide and Cadden Keyes, the latter of whom he says went to California.   They met the advance Oregon caravan about 150 miles west of Fort Laramie, and counted in all for Oregon and California (excepting ours) 478 wagons. There is in our company over 40 wagons, making 518 in all, and there are said to be yet 20 behind. To-morrow we cross the river, and by reckoning will be over 200 miles from Fort Laramie, where we intend to stop and repair our wagon wheels. They are nearly all loose, and I am afraid we will have to stop sooner, if there can be found wood suitable to heat the tires. There is no wood here, and our women and children are out now gathering "buffalo chips" to burn in order to do the cooking These chips burn well.

MRS. GEORGE DONNER.

At Fort Laramie a portion of the Donner Party celebrated the Fourth of July, 1846. Arriving there on the evening of the third, they pitched camp somewhat earlier than usual, and prepared a grand dinner for the Fourth. At the Fort were a large party of Sioux who were on the war-path against the Snakes or Pawnees. The Sioux were, perhaps, the most warlike Indian nation on the great prairies, and when dressed in their war paint and mounted on their fleet ponies, presented a truly imposing appearance. The utmost friendliness prevailed, and there was a mutual interchange of gifts and genial courtesies. When the Donner Party pursued their march, and had journeyed half a day from the Fort, they were overtaken and convoyed quite a distance by about three hundred young warriors. The escort rode in pairs alongside the train in true military fashion. Finally halting, they opened ranks, and as the wagons passed, each warrior held in his mouth a green twig or leaf, which was said to be emblematic of peacefulness and good feeling.

The train was never seriously molested by the Sioux. On one occasion, about fifty warriors on horseback surrounded a portion of the train, in which was the Graves family. While generally friendly, a few of the baser sort persisted in attempting to steal, or take by force, trivial articles which struck their fancy. The main body of Indians were encamped about half a mile away, and when the annoyances became too exasperating, W. C. Graves mounted a horse, rode

to the encampment, and notified the Chief of the action of his fol-
lowers.   Seizing an old-fashioned single-barreled shotgun, the Chief
sprang upon his horse and fairly flew over the plain toward the emigrant wagons.   When within about a hundred yards of the train he
attracted attention by giving an Indian whoop, which was so full of
rage and imprecation that the startled warriors forthwith desisted
from their petty persecutions and scattered in every direction like
frightened quail.   One of the would-be marauders was a little tardy
in mounting his pony, and as soon as the Chief got within range the
shotgun was leveled and discharged full at the unruly subject.   Three
of the buckshot entered the pony's side and one grazed the warrior's
leg.   As if satisfied that his orders to treat the emigrants in a friendly
manner would not be again disregarded, the Chief wheeled his horse
about, and in the most grave and stately manner rode back to his
encampment.

On another occasion, Mary Graves, who was a very beautiful
young lady, was riding on horseback accompanied by her brother.
They were a little in the rear of the train, and a band of Sioux Indians
becoming enamored with the maiden, offered to purchase her.   They
made very handsome offers, but the brother not being disposed to
accept, one of the Indians seized the bridle of the girl's horse and
attempted to carry her away captive.   Perhaps the attempt was made
in half jest.   At all events the bridle was promptly dropped when
the brother leveled his rifle at the savage.

On the 20th of July, 1846, George Donner was elected Captain of
the train at the Little Sandy River.   From that time forward it was
known as the Donner Party.

One incident, not at all unusual to a trip across the plains, is point-
edly described in a letter written by C. T. Stanton to his brother, Sidney Stanton, now of Cazenovia, New York.   The incident alluded to
is the unfriendliness and want of harmony so liable to exist between
different companies, and between members of the same company.
From one of Mr. Stanton's letters the following extract is made:

"At noon we passed Boggs' company on the Sweetwater; a mile
further up the river, Dunlavy's; a mile further, West's; and about two

miles beyond that, was Dunbar's. We encamped about half way between the two latter. Thus, within five miles were encamped five companies. At Indian Creek, twenty miles from Independence, these five companies all constituted one, but owing to dissensions and quarreling they became broken into fragments. Now, by accident, we all again once more meet and grasp the cordial hand; old enmities are forgot, and nothing but good feeling prevails. * * * * * The next morning we got rather a late start, owing to a difference of opinion arising in our company as to whether we should lay by or go ahead. Those wishing to lay by were principally young men who wished to have a day's hunting among the buffaloes, and there were also a few families out of meat who wished to lay in a supply before they left the buffalo country. A further reason was urged that the cattle were nearly fagged out by hard travel, and that they would not stand the journey unless we stopped and gave them rest. On the other side it was contended that if we stopped here the other companies would all get ahead, the grass would all be eaten off by their thousand head of cattle, and that consequently, when we came along our cattle would starve. The go-ahead party finally ruled and we rolled out."

As will presently be seen, the dissension existing in the company, and the petty differences of opinion and interest, were the fundamental causes of the calamities which befell the Donner Party.

When the company was near Fort Bridger, Edward Breen's leg was broken by a fall from a horse. His mother refused to permit amputation, or rather left the question to Edward's decision, and of course, boy-like, he refused to have the operation performed. Contrary to expectation, the bone knitted, and in a month he walked without a crutch.

At Fort Bridger, which was at this time a mere camp or trading post, the party heard much commendation bestowed upon a new route via Salt Lake. This route passed along the southern shore of the Lake, and rejoined the old Fort Hall emigrant road on the Humboldt. It was said to shorten the distance three hundred miles. The new route was known as the Hastings Cut-off, and was named after the famous hunter and trapper L. W. Hastings, who was even then piloting a small company over the cut-off. The large trains delayed for three or four days at Fort Bridger, debating as to the best course to pursue. It is claimed that but for the earnest advice and solicitation of Bridger and Vasquez, who had charge of the fort, the entire party would have continued by the accustomed route. These men had a direct interest in the Hastings Cut-off, as they furnished the emigrants with supplies, and had employed Hastings to pilot the first company over the road to Salt Lake.

After mature deliberation, the party divided, the greater portion going by Fort Hall and reaching California in safety. With the large train, which journeyed the old road, this narrative is no longer interested. Eighty-seven persons, however, took the Hastings Cut-off. Their names are included in the ninety mentioned in the preceding chapter. Mrs. Sarah Keyes having died, and Lewis and Salvador not being with the train. For several days the party traveled without much difficulty. They reached Weber River near the head of the well known Weber Canyon. At the first crossing of this river, on the 3d of August, they found a letter from Hastings stuck in the split of a stick, informing them that the road down the Weber Canyon was in a terrible condition, and that it was doubtful if the sixty-six wagons which Lansford W. Hastings was then piloting through the canyon would ever succeed in reaching the plain. In the letter Hastings advised all emigrants to avoid the canyon road, and pursue over the mountains a course which he faintly outlined. In order to obtain further information, and, if possible, to induce Hastings to return and act as guide, Messrs. Reed, Stanton, and Pike were sent forward to overtake the advance company. This was accomplished after a fatiguing trip, which so exhausted the horses of Stanton and Pike that these gentlemen were unable to return to the Donner Party. Hastings was overtaken at a point near the southern end of Great Salt Lake, and came back with Reed to the foot of the bluffs overlooking the present city of Salt Lake. Here he declared that he must return to the company he was piloting, and despite the urgent entreaties of Reed, decided that it was his duty to start back the next morning. He finally consented, however, to ascend to the summit of the Wahsatch Mountains, from which he endeavored, as best he could, to point out the direction in which the wagons must travel from the head of the Weber Canyon. Reed proceeded alone on the route indicated, taking notes of the country and occasionally blazing trees to assist him in retracing the course.

Wm. G. Murphy (now of Marysville), says that the wagons remained in the meadows at the head of Weber Canyon until Reed's return. They then learned that the train which preceded them had been compelled to travel very slowly down the Weber River, filling in many irregular places with brush and dirt. That at last they had reached a place where vast perpendicular pillars of rock approached so closely on either side that the river had barely space to flow between, and just here the water plunged over a precipice. To lower the wagons down this precipice had been a dreadful task.

The Donner Party unanimously decided to take across the moun tains in a more direct line toward Salt Lake. They soon found rolling highlands and small summit valleys on the divide between Weber River and Salt Lake. Following down one of the small streams, they found a varying, irregular canyon, down which they passed, filling its small stream with brush and rocks, crossing and recrossing it, making roads, breaking and mending wagons, until three weeks time had expired. The entire country was heavily covered with timber and underbrush. When the party arrived at the outlet of this stream into Salt Lake Valley, they found it utterly impassable. It was exceedingly narrow, and was filled with huge rocks from the cliffs on either side. Almost all the oxen in the train were necessary in drawing each wagon out of the canyon and up the steep over-hanging mountain. While in this canyon, Stanton and Pike came up to the company. These gentlemen encountered great hardships after their horses gave out, and were almost starved to death when they reached the train.

Instead of reaching Salt Lake in a week, as had been promised, the party were over thirty days in making the trip. No words can describe what they endured on this Hastings Cut-off. The terrible delay was rendering imminent the dangers which awaited them on the Sierra Nevadas. At last, upon ascending the steep rugged mountain before mentioned, the vision of Great Salt Lake, and the extensive plains surrounding it, burst upon their enraptured gaze. All were wild with joy and gratitude for their deliverance from the terrible struggle through which they had just passed, and all hoped for a prosperous, peaceful journey over pleasant roads throughout the remainder of the trip to California. Alas! there were trials in the way compared with which their recent struggles were insignificant. But for the fatal delay caused by the Hastings Cut-off, all would have been well, but now the Summer was passed, their teams and themselves were well-nigh exhausted, and their slender stock of provisions nearly consumed.

CHAPTER III.

A Grave of Salt—Abandoned on the Desert—A Night of Horror—The Mirage—
"Cacheing" Goods—A Cry for Relief—Two Heroic Volunteers—A Perilous
Journey.

THE beautiful valley of Great Salt Lake contained little of gladness for the Donner Party. They encamped by the lake on the 3d or 4th of September, 1846. The beautiful Summer had vanished, and Autumn had commenced tinting, with crimson and gold, the foliage on the Wahsatch Mountains. Encamped near the shore of Great Salt Lake, the party buried the second victim claimed by death. This time it was a poor consumptive named Halloran. Without friend or kinsman, Halloran had joined the train and was traveling to California in hopes that a change of climate might effect a cure. Alas! for the poor Irishman, when the leaves began to fall from the trees his spirit winged its flight to the better land. He died in the wagon of Captain George Donner, his head resting in Mrs. Tamsen Donner's lap. It was at sundown. The wagons had just halted for the night. The train had driven up slowly out of respect to the dying emigrant. Looking up into Mrs. Donner's face, he said, "I die happy." Almost while speaking, he died. In return for the many kindnesses he had received during the journey, he left Mr. Donner such property as he possessed, including about fifteen hundred dollars in coin. Hon. Jas. F. Breen, of South San Juan writes: "Halloran's body was buried in a bed of almost pure salt, beside the grave of one who had perished in the preceding train. It was said at the time that bodies thus deposited would not decompose, on account of the preservative properties of the salt. Soon after his burial, his trunk was opened, and Masonic papers and regalia bore witness to the fact that Mr. Halloran was a member of the Masonic Order. James F. Reed, Milton Elliott, and perhaps one or two others in the train also belonged to the mystic tie."

On the 6th day of September they reached a meadow in a valley called "Twenty Wells," as there were that number of wells of various sizes, from six inches to several feet in diameter. The water in these wells rose even with the surface of the ground, and when it was drawn out the wells soon refilled. The water was cold and pure, and peculiarly welcome after the saline plains and alkaline pools they had just passed. Wells similar to these were found during the entire journey of the following day, and the country through which they were passing abounded in luxuriant grass. Reaching the confines of the Salt Lake Desert, which lies southwest of the Lake, they laid in, as they supposed, an ample supply of water and grass. This desert had been represented by Bridger and Vasquez as being only about fifty miles wide. Instead, for a distance of seventy-five miles there was neither water nor grass, but everywhere, a dreary, desolate alkaline waste. Verily, it was—

> "A region of drought, where no river glides,
> Nor rippling brook with osiered sides;
> Where sedgy pool, nor bubbling fount,
> Nor tree, nor cloud, nor misty mount
> Appears to refresh the aching eye,
> But the barren earth and the burning sky,
> And the blank horizon round and round
> Spread, void of living sight or sound."

When the company had been on the desert two nights and one day, Mr. Reed volunteered to go forward and if possible to discover water. His hired teamsters were attending to his teams and wagons

during his absence.   At a distance of perhaps twenty miles he found
the desired water, and hastened to return to the train.   Meantime
there was intense suffering in the party.   Cattle were giving out and
lying down helplessly on the burning sand, or phrenzied with thirst
were straying away into the desert.   Having made preparations for
only fifty miles of desert, several persons came near perishing of
thirst, and cattle were utterly powerless to draw the heavy wagons.
Reed was gone some twenty hours.   During this time his teamsters
had done the wisest thing possible, unhitched the oxen and started
to drive them ahead until water was reached.   It was their intention, of course, to return and get the three wagons and the family
which they had necessarily abandoned on the desert.   Reed passed his
teamsters during the night, and hastened to the relief of his deserted
family.   One of his teamster's horses gave out before morning and
laid down, and while the man's companions were attempting to raise
him, the oxen, rendered unmanageable by their great thirst, disappeared in the desert.   There were eighteen of these oxen.   It is
probable they scented water, and with the instincts of their nature
started out to reach it.   They never were found, and Reed and his
family, consisting of nine persons, were left destitute in the midst of
the desert, eight hundred miles from California.   Near morning,
entirely ignorant of the calamity which had befallen him in the loss
of his cattle, he reached his family.   All day long they looked and
waited in vain for the returning teamsters.   All the rest of the company
had driven ahead and the majority had reached water.   Toward night
the situation grew desperate.   The scanty supply of water left with the
family was almost gone, and another day on the desert would mean
death to all he held dear.   Their only way left was to set out on foot.
He took his youngest child in his arms and the family started to
walk the twenty miles.   During this dreadful night some of the
younger children became so exhausted that, regardless of scoldings
or encouragements, they lay down on the bleak sands.   Even rest,
however, seemed denied the little sufferers, for a chilling wind began
sweeping over the desert, and despite their weariness and anguish,
they were forced to move forward.   At one time during the night

the horror of the situation was changed to intense fright. Through the darkness came a swift rushing animal, which Reed soon recognized as one of his young steers. It was crazed and frenzied with thirst, and for some moments seemed bent upon dashing into the frightened group. Finally, however, it plunged madly away into the night, and was seen no more. Reed suspected the calamity which had prevented the return of the teamsters, but at the moment, the imminent peril surrounding his wife and children banished all thought of worrying about anything but their present situation. God knows what would have become of them had they not soon after daylight discovered the wagon of Jacob Donner. They were received kindly by his family, and conveyed to where the other members of the party were camped. For six or eight days the entire company remained at this spot. Every effort was made to find Reed's lost cattle. Almost every man in the train was out in the desert, searching in all directions. This task was attended with both difficulty and danger; for when the sun shone the atmosphere appeared to distort and magnify objects so that at the distance of a mile every stone or bush would appear the size of an ox. Several of the men came near dying for want of water during this search. The desert mirage disclosed against the horizon, clear, distinct, and perfectly outlined rocks, mountain peaks, and tempting lakelets. Each jagged cliff, or pointed rock, or sharply curved hilltop, hung suspended in air as perfect and complete as if photographed on the sky. Deceived, deluded by these mirages, in spite of their better judgment, several members of the company were led far out into the pathless depths of the desert.

The outlook for Reed was gloomy enough. One cow and one ox were the only stock he had remaining. The company were getting exceedingly impatient over the long delay, yet be it said to their honor, they encamped on the western verge of the desert until every hope of finding Reed's cattle was abandoned. Finally, F. W. Graves and Patrick Breen each lent an ox to Mr. Reed, and by yoking up his remaining cow and ox, he had two yoke of cattle. "Cacheing," or concealing such of his property on the desert, as could not be placed in one wagon, he hitched the two yoke of cattle to this wagon and proceeded on the journey. The word cache occurs so frequently in this history that a brief definition of the interesting process of cacheing might not be amiss. The cache of goods or valuables was generally made in a wagon bed, if one, as in the present instance, was to be abandoned. A square hole, say six feet in depth, was dug in the earth, and in the bottom of this the box or wagon bed containing the articles was placed. Sand, soil, or clay of the proper stratum was filled in upon this, so as to just cover the box from sight. The ground was then tightly packed or trampled, to make it resemble, as much as possible, the earth in its natural state. Into the remaining hole would be placed such useless articles as could be spared, such as old tins, cast-off clothing, broken furniture, etc., and upon these the earth was thrown until the surface of the ground was again level. These precautions were taken to prevent the Indians from discovering and appropriating the articles cached. It was argued that the Indians when digging down would come to the useless articles, and not thinking there was treasure further down would abandon the task. "But," says Hon. James F. Breen, in speaking on this subject, "I have been told by parties who have crossed the plains, that in no case has the Indian been deceived by the emigrant's silent logic." The Indians would leave nothing underground, not even the dead bodies buried from time to time. One of the trains in advance of the Donner Party buried two men in one grave, and succeeding parties found each of the bodies unearthed, and were compelled to repeat the last sad rites of burial.

Before the Donner Party started from the Desert camp, an inventory of the provisions on hand was accurately taken, and an estimate was made of the quantity required for each family, and it was found that there was not enough to carry the emigrants through to California. As if to render more emphatic the terrible situation of the party, a storm came during their last night at the camp, and in the morning the hill-tops were white with snow. It was a dreadful reminder of the lateness of the season, and the bravest hearts quailed before the horrors they knew must await them. A solemn council was held.   It was decided that some one must leave the train, press eagerly forward to California, and obtaining a supply of provisions, return and meet the party as far back on the route as possible.   It was a difficult undertaking, and perilous in the extreme.   A call was made for volunteers, and after a little reflection two men offered their services.   "Two men?"   They were heroes!   Heroes of the truest, noblest, grandest stamp.   One was Wm. McCutchen, who had joined the train from Missouri, and the other was C. T. Stanton, of Chicago, a man who afterwards proved himself possessed of the sublimest heroism.   Taking each a horse, they received the tearful, prayerful farewells of the doomed company, and set out upon their solitary journey.

Would they return?   If they reached the peaceful, golden valleys of California, would they turn back to meet danger, and storms, and death, in order to bring succor to those on the dreary desert? McCutchen might come, because he left dear ones with the train, but would Stanton return?   Stanton was young and unmarried. There were no ties or obligations to prompt his return, save his plighted word and the dictates of honor and humanity.   These men were sent out as the "forlorn hope" of the emigrants.   We will soon see whether they performed their sacred mission.

They bore letters from the Donner Party to Captain Sutter, who was in charge at Sutter's Fort.   These letters were prayers for relief, and it was believed would secure assistance from the generous old Captain.   Every eye folowed Stanton and McCutchen until they disappeared in the west.   Soon afterward the train resumed its toilsome march.

CHAPTER IV

IFE, thirty-three years ago, was not vastly different from life now-a-days. It was impossible that so large a train could cross the great plains without the occurrence of love episodes. Perhaps the tenderest and most sacred of these in the Donner Party was the betrothal of John Snyder and Mary Graves. Mary was one of the sweetest and bravest girls in the company, and was as good and true as she was sweet. Every one knew of the engagement, and every one heartily approved. Whether during the long horseback rides ahead of the train, or amidst the young folks, clambering over the cliffs and cutting their names in the rocks, or yet in the joyous circle about the evening camp-fire, John and Mary were ever and always the happiest couple in all the train. The weariest day was brightened by visions of the little home they would build in the land of the sunset. They had been playmates from childhood; had come from the same town in Illinois, and Snyder drove one of Mr. Graves' teams. Always near each other, every wondrous landscape, every charming cloud picture, every dainty, unfamiliar wild flower, was appreciated the more because seen by both.

John Snyder was a young man, not over twenty-three years old.
He was tall, straight, and of erect, manly carriage, and his habits of
life as a frontiersman developed him into a muscular and athletic
being. He excelled and led in all the out-door sports most in favor
with Western men, such as jumping, running and wrestling. His
manner was gentle, retired and timid to a degree verging on bash-
fulness, until roused by the influence of passion. The lion in the
man was dormant until evoked by the fiercer emotions. His com-
plexion was dark, but as you studied his face you could not repress
the suspicion that Nature had marked him for a blonde, and that
constant exposure to the wind and sun and rain of the great plains
of the West had wrought the color change, and the conviction was
strong that the change was an improvement on Nature. His features
were cast in a mould of great beauty—such beauty as we seldom
look for in a man. He was never moody, despondent, or cast down,
and at all times, and under all circumstances, possessed the faculty
of amusing himself and entertaining others. In the evening camp,
when other amusements failed, or when anticipated troubles depressed
the spirits of the travelers, it was his custom to remove the "hind-
gate" of his wagon, lay it on the ground and thereon perform the
"clog-dance," "Irish jigs," the "pigeon wing," and other fantastic
steps. Many an evening the Donner Party were prevented from
brooding over their troubles by the boyish antics of the light-hearted
youth.

His *fiancé*, Mary Graves, was about nineteen years old. She was
a very beautiful girl, of tall and slender build, and exceptionally
graceful carriage. Her features, in their regularity, were of classic
Grecian mould. Her eyes were dark, bright and expressive. A
fine mouth and perfect set of teeth, added to a luxuriant growth of
dark, rebelliously wavy hair, completed an almost perfect picture of
lovely girlhood.

Just here another character should be prominently introduced.
It is the character of a man who was tender, generous, heroic, and
whose qualities of true nobility shone brilliantly throughout a long

life of usefulness, despite the shadow cast by the sad occurrence narrated in this chapter.

The name of James F. Reed is intimately interwoven with the history of the Donner Party. Indeed, in the Illinois papers of 1846–7 the company was always termed the "Reed and Donner Party." This title was justly conferred at the time, because he was one of the leading spirits in the organization of the enterprise. In order to understand the tragedy which produced the death of John Snyder, and the circumstances resulting therefrom, the reader must become better acquainted with the character of Mr. Reed.

The following brief extract is from "Powers' Early Settlers of Sangamon County": "James Frazier Reed was born Nov. 14, 1800, in County Armagh, Ireland. His ancestors were of noble Polish birth, who chose exile rather than submission to the Russian power, and settled in the north of Ireland. The family name was originally Reednoski, but in process of time the Polish termination of the name was dropped, and the family was called Reed. James F. Reed's mother's name was Frazier, whose ancestors belonged to Clan Frazier, of Scottish history. Mrs. Reed and her son, James F., came to America when he was a youth, and settled in Virginia. He remained there until he was twenty, when he left for the lead mines of Illinois, and was engaged in mining until 1831, when he came to Springfield, Sangamon County, Illinois."

Among the papers of Mr. Reed is a copy of the muster roll of a company which enlisted in the Blackhawk war, and in this roll are the names of Abraham Lincoln, Stephen A. Douglass, and James F. Reed. At the termination of this war, Mr. Reed returned to Springfield, engaged in the manufacture of cabinet furniture, and amassed a considerable fortune. He was married in 1834 to Mrs. Margaret, Backenstoe, whose maiden name was Keyes. The death of his wife's mother, Mrs. Sarah Keyes, has already been mentioned as occurring on the Big Blue River, near Manhattan, Kansas.

During the progress of the train, Mr. Reed was at all times a prominent, active member. Full of life and enthusiasm, fearless of danger, he was ready at all times to risk his life for the company's welfare.   On the desert, we have seen that his lonely expedition in search of water cost him his valuable oxen, and left him and his family almost destitute.

The deplorable affair about to be narrated was only the natural outgrowth of the trying circumstances in which the company were placed.   The reader must bear in mind that many petty causes combined to produce discord and dissension among the members of the Donner Party.   Coming from so many different States, being of different nationalities and modes of thought, delayed on the road much longer than was expected, rendered irritable by the difficulties encountered on the journey, annoyed by losses of stock, fearful of unknown disasters on the Sierras, and already placed on short allowances of provisions, the company was decidedly inharmonious.

The train had reached Gravelly Ford, on the Humboldt.   Already they were beginning to scan eagerly the western plain, in hopes of discovering the relief party from Sutter's Fort.   Occasionally a wagon would need repairing.   Occasionally there would be a brief halt to rest and recruit the jaded cattle.   The Indians had stolen two of Mr. Graves' oxen, and a couple of days later had stolen one of the horses.

In traveling, the Donner Party observed this rule: if a wagon drove in the lead one day, it should pass back to the rear on the succeeding day.   This system of alternating allowed each his turn in leading the train.   On this 5th of October, 1846, F. W. Graves was ahead, Jay Fosdick second, John Snyder third, and the team of J. F. Reed fourth.   Milton Elliott was driving Reed's team.   Arriving at the foot of a steep, sandy hill, the party was obliged to "double teams," that is, to hitch five or six yoke of oxen to one wagon. Elliott and Snyder interchanged hot words over some difficulty about the oxen.   Fosdick had attached his team to Graves' and had drawn Graves' wagon up the hill.   Snyder being nettled at something Elliott had said, declared that his team could pull up alone.   During the excitement Snyder made use of very bad language, and was beating his cattle over the head with his whip-stock.   One account says that Reed's team and Snyder's became tangled.   At all events,

Snyder was very much enraged. Reed had been off hunting on horseback, and arriving at this moment, remonstrated with Snyder for beating the cattle, and at the same time offered him the assistance of his team. Snyder refused the proffered aid, and used abusive language toward both Reed and Elliott. Reed attempted to calm the enraged man. Both men were of fiery, passionate dispositions, and words began to multiply rapidly. When Reed saw that trouble was likely to occur, he said something about waiting until they got up the hill and settling this matter afterwards. Snyder evidently construed this to be a threat, and with an oath replied, "We will settle it now." As Snyder uttered these words he struck Reed a blow on the head with the butt end of his heavy whip-stock. This blow was followed in rapid succession by a second, and a third. As the third stroke descended, Mrs. Reed ran between her husband and the furious man, hoping to prevent the blow. Each time the whip-stock descended on Reed's head it had cut deep gashes. He was blinded with the blood which streamed from his wounds, and dazed and stunned by the terrific force of the blows. He saw the cruel whipstock uplifted, and knew that his wife was in danger, but had only time to cry "John! John!" when down came the stroke full upon Mrs. Reed's head and shoulders. The next instant John Snyder was staggering, speechless and death-stricken. Reed's hunting-knife had pierced his left breast, severing the first and second ribs and entering the left lung.

No other portion of the History of the Donner Party, as contributed by the survivors, has been so variously stated as this Reed-Snyder affair. Five members of the party, now living, claim to have been eye-witnesses. The version of two of these, Mrs. J. M. Murphy and Mrs. Frank Lewis, is the one here published. In the theory of self-defense they are corroborated by all the early published accounts. This theory was first advanced in Judge J. Quinn Thornton's work in 1849, and has never been disputed publicly until within the last two or three years. Due deference to the valuable assistance rendered by Wm. G. Murphy, of Marysville, and W. C. Graves, of Calistoga, demands mention of the fact that their accounts differ in

important respects from the one given above.   This is not surprising
in view of the thirty-three years which have elapsed since the occurrence.   The history of criminal jurisprudence justifies the assertion
that eye-witnesses of any fatal difficulty differ materially in regard to
important particulars, even when their testimony is taken immediately
after the difficulty.   It is not strange, therefore, that after the lapse
of an ordinary lifetime a dozen different versions should have been
contributed by the survivors concerning this unfortunate tragedy.
James F. Reed, after nearly a quarter of a century of active public
life in California, died honored and respected.   During his lifetime
this incident appeared several times in print, and was always sub-
stantially as given in this chapter.   With the single exception of a
series of articles contributed to the Healdsburg Flag by W. C.
Graves, two or three years ago, no different account has ever been
published.   This explanatory digression from the narrative is deemed
necessary out of respect to the two gentlemen who conscientiously
disagree with Mrs. Murphy and Mrs. Lewis.   On all other important
subjects the survivors are harmonious or reconcilable.

W. C. Graves, now of Calistoga, caught the dying man in his
arms, and in a few minutes he was carried a little way up the hill
and laid upon the ground.   Reed immediately regretted the act and
threw the knife from him.   His wife and daughters gathered about
him and began to staunch the blood that flowed from the gashes on
his head.   He gently pushed them aside and went to the assistance
of the dying man.   He and Snyder had always been firm friends,
and Snyder had been most active in securing a team for Reed after
the latter had lost his cattle in the desert.   Snyder expired in about
fifteen minutes, and Reed remained by his side until the last.
Patrick Breen came up, and Snyder said, " Uncle Patrick, I am
dead."   It is not certain that he spoke again, though Reed's friends
claim that he said to Reed, " I am to blame."

Snyder's death fell like a thunderbolt upon the Donner Party.
Camp was immediately pitched, the Reed family being a little
removed, down the hill, from the main body of emigrants.   Reed
felt that he had only acted in defense of his own life and in defense

of the wife he adored. Nevertheless, it was evident that trouble was brewing in the main camp where Snyder's body was lying.

The Reed family were in a sad situation. They commenced the journey with a more costly and complete outfit than the other emigrants, and thereby had incurred the envy of some of their less fortunate companions. They had a fine race horse and good stock, and Virginia had a beautiful pony of her own, and was fond of accompanying her father on his horseback excursions. From these and other circumstances, the Reeds had acquired the name of being "aristocratic." Ordinarily, this is a term which would excite a smile, but on this dreadful day it had its weight in inflaming the minds of the excited emigrants. On the desert, Reed had cached many valuable articles, but all his provisions had been distributed among his companions. This, however, was forgotten in the turbulent camp, and the desolate, destitute family could plainly catch the sound of voices clamoring for Reed's death.

Meantime, Virginia Reed was dressing the wounds on her father's head. Mrs. Reed was overwhelmed with grief and apprehension, and the father came to Virginia for assistance. This brave little woman was only twelve years old, yet in this and all other acts of which there is a record, she displayed a nerve and skillfulness which would have done credit to a mature woman. The cuts in Reed's scalp were wide and deep. Indeed, the scars remained to his dying day. In San Jose, long years afterwards, as James F. Reed lay dead, the gentle breeze from an open window softly lifted and caressed his gray hair, disclosing plainly the scars left by these ugly wounds.

Reed entertained none but the friendliest sentiments toward Snyder. Anxious to do what he could for the dead, he offered the boards of his wagon-bed from which to make a coffin for Snyder. This offer, made with the kindliest, most delicate feeling, was rejected by the emigrants. At the funeral, Reed stood sorrowfully by the grave, until the last clod was placed above the man who had been his best friend. A council was held by the members of the company. A council to decide upon Reed's fate. It was in the nature of a court, all-powerful, from whose decision there was no appeal. Breathlessly the fond wife and affectionate children awaited the verdict. The father was idolized by the mother and the little ones, and was their only stay and support.

The friendship of the Donner Party for John Snyder, the conflicting and distorted accounts of the tragedy, and the personal enmity of certain members of the company toward Reed, resulted in a decree that he should be banished from the train. The feeling ran so high, that at one time the end of a wagon-tongue was propped up .with an ox yoke by some of the emigrants with the intention of hanging Reed thereon, but calmer counsel prevailed.

When the announcement was communicated to Reed that he was to be banished, he refused to comply with the decree. Conscious that he had only obeyed the sacred law of self-defense, he refused to accede to an unjust punishment. Then came the wife's pleadings! Long and earnestly Mrs. Reed reasoned and begged and prayed with her husband. All was of no avail until she urged him to remember the want and destitution in which they 'and the entire company were already participants. If he remained and escaped violence at the hands of his enemies, he might nevertheless see his children starve before his eyes, and be helpless to aid them. But if he would go forward, if he would reach California, he could return with provisions, and meet them on the mountains at that point on the route where they would be in greatest need. It was a fearful struggle, but finally the mother's counsels prevailed.

Prior to setting out upon his gloomy journey, Mr. Reed made the company solemnly promise to care for his family. Walter Herron, a member of the party, was two days in advance of the main train with the wagons of George and Jacob Donner, and concluded to accompany Reed to California.

It was contemplated that Reed should go out into the wilderness alone, and with neither food nor ammunition. Happily this part of the programme was thwarthed. The faithful Virginia, in company with Milton Elliot, followed Mr. Reed after he had started, and carried him his gun and ammunition. The affectionate girl also managed to carry some crackers to him, although she and all the company were even then on short allowance.

The sad parting between Reed and his family, and the second parting with the devoted Virginia, we pass over in silence. James F. Reed, Jr., only five years old, declared that he would go with his father, and assist him in obtaining food during the long journey. Even the baby, only two and a half years old, would fret and worry every time the family sat down to their meals, lest father should find nothing to eat on his difficult way. Every day the mother and daughters would eagerly search for the letter Mr. Reed was sure to leave in the top of some bush, or in a split stick by the wayside. When he succeeded in killing geese or ducks, as he frequently did along the Humboldt and Truckee, he would scatter the feathers about his camping ground, that his family might see that he was supplied with food. It is hardly necessary to mention that Mrs. Reed and the children regarded the father's camping places as hallowed ground, and as often as possible kindled their evening fires in the same spot where his had been kindled.

But a day came when they found no more letters, no further traces of the father. Was he dead? Had the Indians killed him? Had he starved by the way? No one could answer, and the mother's cheek grew paler and her dear eyes grew sadder and more hopeless, until Virginia and Patty both feared that she too, was going to leave them. Anxious, grief-stricken, filled with the belief that her husband was dead, poor Mrs. Reed was fast dying of a broken heart. But suddenly all her life, and energy, and determination were again aroused into being by a danger that would have crushed a nature less noble. A danger that is the most terrible, horrible, that ever tortured human breast: a danger—that her children, her babes, must starve to death !

CHAPTER V.

Great Hardships—An Entire Company Compelled to Walk—Abandoned to Die—Arrival of C. T. Stanton—A Temporary Relief—A Fatal Accident—The Sierra Nevadas—Imprisoned in Snow—Struggles for Freedom—A Hopeless Situation—Digging for Cattle in Snow—A Thrilling Sketch of a Solitary Winter—Fishing for Trout.

TARVATION now stared the emigrants in the face. The shortest allowance capable of supporting life was all that was portioned to any member of the company. At times, some were forced to do without food for a day or more, until game was procured. The poor cattle were also in a pitiable condition. Owing to the lateness of the season, the grass was exceedingly scanty and of a poor quality. Frequently the water was bad, and filled with alkali and other poisonous deposits. George Donner, Jacob Donner, Wolfinger, and others, lost cattle at various points along the Humboldt. Mr. Breen lost a fine mare. The Indians were constantly hovering around the doomed train, ready to steal cattle, but too cowardly to make any open hostile attack. Arrows were shot into several of the oxen by Indians who slipped up near them during the night-time. At midnight, on the 12th of October, the party reached the sink of the Humboldt. The cattle, closely guarded, were turned out to graze and recruit their wasted strength. About dawn on the morning of the 13th, the guard came into camp to breakfast. During the night nothing had occurred to cause the least apprehension, and no indications of Indians had been observed. Imagine the consternation in camp when it was discovered that during the temporary absence of the guard, twenty-one head of cattle were stolen by the redskins. This left the company in terribly destitute circumstances. All had to walk who were able. Men, women and children were forced to travel on foot all day long, and in many cases were compelled to carry heavy burdens in order to lessen the loads drawn by the weary cattle. Wm. G. Murphy remembers distinctly seeing his brother carrying a copper camp-kettle upon his head. The Graves family, the Breens, the Donners, the Murphys, the Reeds, all walked beside the wagons until overpowered with fatigue. The men became exhausted much sooner, as a rule, than the women. Only the sick, the little children, and the utterly exhausted, were ever allowed to ride. Eddy and his wife had lost all their cattle, and each carried one of their children and such personal effects as they were able. Many in the train were without shoes, and had to travel barefooted over the weary sands, and flinty, sharp-edged stones.

On the 9th of October a death had resulted from this necessity of having to walk. It was a case of desertion, which, under other circumstances, would have been unpardonably heartless. An old man named Hardcoop was traveling with Keseberg. He was a cutler by trade, and had a son and daughter in the city of Antwerp, in Belgium. It is said he owned a farm near Cincinnati, Ohio, and intended, after visiting California, to dispose of this farm, and with the proceeds return to Antwerp, for the purpose of spending his declining years with his children. He was a man of nearly three-score years, and the hardships of the journey had weakened his trembling limbs, and broken down his health. Sick, feeble, helpless as he was, this old man was compelled to walk with the others. At last, when his strength gave way, he was forced to lie down by the roadside to perish of cold and hunger. Who can picture the agony, the horror, the dreary desolation of such a death? The poor old man walked until his feet actually burst!—walked until he

3

sank utterly exhausted by the roadside! It was a terrible death! To see the train disappear in the distance—to know he was abandoned to die of exposure and starvation—to think that the wolves would devour his flesh and gnaw his bones—to lie down on the great desert, hungry, famished, and completely prostrated by fatigue—to meet death thus, is too dreadful to contemplate.

Keseberg made no attempt to return and find the poor old fellow. This, however, is partially excused by the overwhelming dangers which now threatened the entire company. When the train learned of Hardcoop's abandonment, it was too late to succor the unfortunate outcast.

About the 14th of October, beyond the present site of Wadsworth, another tragedy occurred. Wolfinger, who was supposed to be quite wealthy, was in the rear of the train, traveling with Keseberg. At nightfall, neither of the Germans made their appearance. It happened that both their wives had walked ahead, and were with the emigrants. Considering it suspicious that the men did not arrive, and fearing some evil had befallen them, a party returned to ascertain the cause of the delay. Before proceeding far, however, Keseberg was met, traveling leisurely along. He assured them that Wolfinger was only a little way behind, and would be along in a few moments. Reassured by this information, the party returned with Keseberg to camp, and awaited the arrival of Wolfinger. The night passed, and the missing man had not appeared. Mrs. Wolfinger was nearly frantic. She was a tall, queenly looking lady, of good birth and much refinement. She was recently from Germany, and understood but little English, yet she was evidently a well-bred lady. Nearly all the survivors remember the elegant dresses and costly jewelry she wore during the first part of the journey. Her grief at her husband's disappearance was so heartrending that three young men at last consented to start back in the morning and endeavor to find Wolfinger. W. C. Graves, from whom this information is obtained, was one of the three who returned. Five miles back the wagon was found standing in the road. The oxen had been unhitched, but were still chained together, and were quietly grazing at a little distance.

There were no signs of Indians, but Wolfinger was not to be found. At the time, it was strongly conjectured that Keseberg had murdered Wolfinger for his money, and had concealed the body. This was doubtless unjust, for when Joseph Rhinehart was dying, some weeks later, in George Donner's tent, he confessed that he (Rhinehart), had something to do with the murder of Wolfinger. The men hitched the oxen to the wagon, and drove on until they overtook the emigrants, who, owing to the dangers by which they were encompassed, felt compelled to pursue their onward journey. The team was given to Mrs. Wolfinger, and she employed a German by the name of Charles Burger to drive it thereafter. Little was said about the affair at the time. Mrs. Wolfinger supposed the Indians had killed her husband.

On the 19th of October, C. T. Stanton was met returning with provisions. The company was near the present town of Wadsworth. A great rejoicing was held over the brave man's return. McCutchen had been severely ill, and was unable to return with Stanton. But the latter, true to his word, recrossed the Sierras, and met the emigrants at a time when they were on the verge of starvation. He had brought seven mules, five of which were loaded with flour and dried beef. Captain Sutter (God bless him), had furnished these mules and the provisions, together with two Indian vaqueros, without the slightest compensation or security. The Indians, Lewis and Salvador, would assist in caring for the pack-animals, and would also be efficient guides. Without Stanton's aid the entire party would have been lost—not a single soul would have escaped. The provisions, though scant, were sufficient to entirely alter the situation of affairs. Had the party pressed immediately forward, they could have passed the summits before the storms began. For some cause, however, it was concluded to rest the cattle for a few days near the present site of Reno, preparatory to attempting to ascend the difficult Sierras. Three or four days' time was lost. This loss was fatal. The storms on the mountains generally set in about Thanksgiving, or during the latter days of November. The emigrants trusted that

the storm season of 1846 would not begin earlier than usual.   Alas !
the terrible consequences of this mistaken trust !

After the arrival of Stanton, it was still deemed necessary to take
further steps for the relief of the train.   The generosity of Captain
Sutter, as shown to Stanton, warranted them in believing that he
would send still further supplies to the needy emigrants.   Accordingly, two brothers-in-law, William Foster and William Pike, both
brave and daring spirits, volunteered to go on ahead, cross the
summits, and return with provisions as Stanton had done.   Both
men had families, and both were highly esteemed in the company.
At the encampment near Reno, while they were busily preparing
to start, the two men were cleaning or loading a pistol.   It was an
old-fashioned " pepper-box."   It happened, while they were exam
ining it, that wood was called for to replenish the fire.   One of the
men offered to procure it, and in order to do so, handed the pistol
to the other.   Everybody knows that the "pepper-box" is a very
uncertain weapon.   Somehow, in the transfer, the pistol was discharged.   William Pike was fatally wounded, and died in about
twenty minutes.   Mrs. Pike was left a widow, with two small children.   The youngest, Catherine, was a babe of only a few months old,
and Naomi was only three years of age.   The sadness and distress
occasioned by this mournful accident, cast a gloom over the entire
company, and seemed an omen of the terrible fate which over-
shadowed the Donner Party.

Generally, the ascent of the Sierras brought joy and gladness to
weary overland emigrants.   To the Donner Party it brought terror
and dismay.   The company had hardly obtained a glimpse of the
mountains, ere the Winter storm clouds began to assemble their
hosts around the loftier crests.   Every day the weather appeared
more ominous and threatening.   The delay at the Truckee Meadows
had been brief, but every day ultimately cost a dozen lives.   On the
23d of October they became thoroughly alarmed at the angry
heralds of the gathering storm, and with all haste resumed the journey.
It was too late!   At Prosser Creek, three miles below Truckee, they
found themselves encompassed with six inches of snow.   On the

summits, the snow was from two to five feet in depth. This was October 28th, 1846. Almost a month earlier than usual, the Sierras had donned their mantle of ice and snow. The party were prisoners. All was consternation. The wildest confusion prevailed. In their eagerness, many went far in advance of the main train. There was little concert of action or harmony of plan. All did not arrive at Donner Lake the same day. Some wagons and families did not reach the lake until the 31st day of October, some never went further than Prosser Creek, while others, on the evening of the 29th, had struggled through the snow, and reached the foot of the precipitous cliffs between the summit and the upper end of the lake. Here, baffled, wearied, disheartened, they turned back to the foot of the lake.

Several times during the days which succeeded, parties attempted to cross the mountain barrier. W. C. Graves says the old emigrant road followed up Cold Stream, and so crossed the dividing ridge. Some wagons were drawn up this old road, almost to the top of the pass, others were taken along the north side of Donner Lake, and far up toward the summit. Some of these wagons never were returned to the lake, but were left imbedded in the snow. These efforts to cross the Sierras were quite desultory and irregular, and there was great lack of harmony and system. Each family or each little group of emigrants acted independently.

At last, one day, a determined and systematic attempt was made to cross the summit. Nearly the entire train was engaged in the work. The road, of course, was entirely obliterated by the snow. Guided only by the general contour of the country, all hands pressed resolutely forward. Here, large bowlders and irregular jutting cliffs would intercept the way; there, dizzy precipices, yawning chasms, and deep irregular canyons would interpose, and anon a bold impassable mountain of rock would rear its menacing front directly across their path. All day long the men and animals floundered through the snow, and attempted to break and trample a road. Just before nightfall they reached the abrupt precipice where the present wagon road intercepts the snow-sheds of the Central

Pacific. Here the poor mules and oxen had been utterly unable to find a foothold on the slippery, snow-covered rocks. All that day it had been raining slightly—a dismal, drizzling, discouraging rain. Most of the wagons had been left at the lake, and the mules and oxen had been packed with provisions and necessary articles. Even at this day, some of the survivors are unable to repress a ripple of merriment as they recall the manner in which the oxen bucked and bellowed when the unaccustomed packs were strapped upon their backs. Stanton had stoutly insisted upon taking the mules over the mountains. Perhaps he did not wish to return to Capt. Sutter without the property which he had borrowed. Many in the train dissented from this proposition, and endeavored to induce the Indians, Lewis and Salvador, to leave Stanton, and guide them over the summits. The Indians realized the imminent danger of each hour's delay, and would probably have yielded to the solicitations of these disaffected parties, had not Stanton made them believe that Capt. Sutter would hang them if they returned to the Fort without the mules. This incident is mentioned to illustrate the great differences of opinion and interest which prevailed. Never, from the moment the party encountered the first difficulties on the Hastings Cut-off until this fatal night in November, did the members of the company ever agree upon any important proposition. This night all decided upon a plan for the morrow. The great and overwhelming danger made them forget their petty animosities, and united them in one harmonious resolve. On the morrow the mules and cattle were all to be slain, and the meat was to be stored away for future emergency. The wagons, with their contents, were to be left at the lake, and the entire party were to cross the summits on foot. Stanton had become perfectly satisfied that the mules could not reach the mountain-top, and readily consented to the proposed plan.

Returning to the lake they sought their weary couches, comforted with the thought that to-morrow should see all the Donner Party safely over the summit. That night a heavy snow fell at the lake. It was a night of untold terror ! The emigrants suffered a thousand deaths. The pitiless snow came down in large, steady masses. All understood that the storm meant death. One of the Indians silently wrapped his blanket about him, and in deepest dejection seated himself beside a tall pine. In this position he passed the entire night, only moving occasionally to keep from being covered with snow. Mrs. Reed spread down a shawl, placed her four children, Virginia, Patty, James, and Thomas thereon, and putting another shawl over them, sat by the side of her babies during all the long hours of darkness. Every little while she was compelled to lift the upper shawl and shake off the rapidly accumulating snow.

With slight interruptions, the storm continued several days. The mules and oxen that had always hovered about camp, were blinded and bewildered by the storm, and straying away, were literally buried alive in the drifts. What pen can describe the horror of the position in which the emigrants found themselves. It was impossible to move through the deep, soft snow, without the greatest effort. The mules were gone, and were never found. Most of the cattle had perished, and were wholly hidden from sight. The few oxen which were found were slaughtered for beef. All were not killed during any one day, but the emigrants gave this business their immediate attention, because aside from the beef and a few slight provisions, the entire party were completely destitute. Mrs. Breen was compelled to attend personally to the slaughtering of their cattle, because her husband was an invalid. This family had by far the largest stock of meat. Too great praise cannot be ascribed to Mrs. Breen for the care and forethought with which she stored up this food for her children. The meat was simply laid away in piles, like cordwood, and by the action of the frost was kept fresh until consumed. Mrs. Reed had no cattle to kill. She succeeded, however, in purchasing two beeves from Mr. Graves, and two from Mr. Breen, pledging herself to pay when the journey was ended. Mr. Eddy also purchased one ox of Mr. Graves.

The flesh of many of the cattle which strayed away, and were buried several feet under the snow, was nevertheless recovered by their owners. It was soon ascertained that the cattle had endeavored to seek shelter from the fury of the storm by getting under the branches of the bushiest trees. Going to these trees, the emigrants would thrust down long poles with sharpened nails in the ends of them. By thus probing about in the snow, the whereabouts of a number of cattle was discovered, and the bodies were speedily dug out of the drifts.

Realizing that the Winter must be passed in the mountains, the emigrants made such preparations as they could for shelter. One cabin was already constructed. It was located about a quarter of a mile below the foot of the lake. It had been built in November, 1844, by Moses Schallenberger, Joseph Foster and Allen Montgomery. Moses Schallenberger now resides three and a half miles from San Jose, and when recently interviewed by Mrs. S. O. Houghton nee Eliza P. Donner, gave a very complete and interesting account of the building of this cabin, and the sufferings endured by his party. This cabin, known as the Breen cabin, is so intimately connected and interwoven with future chapters in the History of the Donner Party, that the following items, taken from Mr. Schallenberger's narration, cannot prove uninteresting :

"Mr. Schallenberger's party reached Donner Lake about the middle of November, 1844, having with them a large quantity of goods for California. Their cattle being very poor, and much fatigued by the journey, the party decided to remain here long enough to build a cabin in which to store their goods until Spring. They also decided to leave some one to look after their stores, while the main portion of the party would push on to the settlement. Foster, Montgomery and Schallenberger built the cabin. Two days were spent in its construction. It was built of pine saplings, and roofed with pine brush and rawhides. It was twelve by fourteen feet, and seven or eight feet high, with a chimney in one end, built "western style." One opening, through which light, air, and the occupants passed, served as a window and door. A heavy fall of snow began the day after the cabin was completed and continued for a number of days. Schallenberger, who was only seventeen years old, volunteered to remain with Foster and Montgomery. The party passed on, leaving very little provisions for the encamped. The flesh of one miserably poor cow was their main dependence, yet the young men were not discouraged. They were accustomed to frontier life, and felt sure they could provide for themselves. Bear and deer seemed abundant in the surrounding mountains. Time passed; the snow continued falling, until it was from ten to fifteen feet deep. The cow was more than half consumed, and the game had been driven out of the mountains by the storms.

"The sojourners in that lonely camp became alarmed at the prospect of the terrible fate which seemed to threaten them, and they determined to find their way across the mountains. They started and reached the summit the first night after leaving their camp. Here, young Schallenberger was taken ill with severe cramps. The following day he was unable to proceed more than a few feet without falling to the ground. It was evident to his companions that he could go no farther. They did not like to leave him, nor did they wish to remain where death seemed to await them. Finally Schallenberger told them if they would take him back to the cabin he would remain there and they could go on. This they did, and after making him as comfortable as possible, they bade him good bye, and he was left alone in that mountain wild. A strong will and an unflinching determination to live through all the threatening dangers, soon raised him from his bed and nerved him to action. He found some steel traps among the goods stored, and with them caught foxes, which constituted his chief or only article of food, until rescued by the returning party, March 1st, 1845."

The Breen family moved into the Schallenberger cabin. Against the west side of this cabin, Keseberg built a sort of half shed into which he and his family entered. The Murphys erected a cabin nearer the lake. The site of this cabin is plainly marked by a large stone about ten or twelve feet high, one side of which rises almost perpendicularly from the ground. Against this perpendicular side the Murphys erected the building which was to shelter them during the Winter. It was about three hundred yards from the shore of Donner Lake, and near the wide marshy outlet. The Graves family built a house close by Donner Creek, and half or three-quarters of a mile further down the stream. These three cabins formed an obtuse triangle. The Breen and Murphy cabins were distant from each other about one hundred and fifty yards. The Donner brothers, Jacob and George, together with their families, camped in Alder Creek Valley, six or seven miles from Donner Lake. They were, if possible, in a worse condition than the others, for they had only brush sheds and their tents to shield them from the wintry weather. Mrs. John App (Leanna C. Donner), of Jamestown, Tuolumne County, writes : "We had no time to build a cabin. The snow came on so suddenly that we had barely time to pitch our tent, and put up a brush shed, as it were, one side of which was open. This brush shed was covered with pine boughs, and then covered with rubber coats, quilts, etc. My uncle, Jacob Donner, and family, also had a tent, and camped near us."

Crowded in their illy-prepared dwellings, the emigrants could not feel otherwise than gloomy and despondent. The small quantity of provisions became so nearly exhausted that it is correct to say they were compelled to live on meat alone, without so much as salt to give it a relish. There was an abundance of beautiful trout in the lake, but no one could catch them. W. C. Graves tells how he went fishing two or three different times, but without success. The lake was not frozen over at first, and fish were frequently seen; but they were too coy and wary to approach such bait as was offered. Soon thick ice covered the water, and after that no one attempted to fish. In fact, the entire party seemed dazed by the terrible calamity which had overtaken them.

CHAPTER VI.

LL knew that death speedily awaited the entire company
unless some could cross over the mountain barrier and
hasten back relief parties.   Out of the list of ninety persons mentioned in the first chapter, only Mrs. Sarah Keyes,
Halloran, Snyder, Hardcoop, Wolfinger, and Pike had
perished, and only three, Messrs. Reed, Herron, and
McCutchen had reached California.   This left eighty-one persons at
the mountain camps.   It was resolved that at the earliest possible moment the strongest and ablest of the party should endeavor to cross
the summits and reach the settlements.   Accordingly, on the 12th
of November, a party of twelve or fifteen persons set out from the
cabins.   It was found impossible, however, to make any considerable
headway in the soft, deep snow, and at midnight they returned to the
cabins.   They had not succeeded in getting more than a mile above
the head of the lake.   In this party were Mr. F. W. Graves and his
two daughters, Mary A. Graves, and Mrs. Sarah Fosdick.   The rest,
with the exception of Jay Fosdick and Wm. H. Eddy, were young,
unmarried men, as for instance, Stanton, Smith, Spitzer, Elliott,
Antoine, John Baptiste, and the two Indians.   It was comparatively

a trifling effort, but it seemed to have the effect of utterly depressing the hopes of several of these men. With no one in the camps dependent upon them, without any ties of relationship, or bonds of affection, these young men were the first to attempt to escape from their prison walls of snow. Failing in this, many of them never again rallied or made a struggle for existence. Not so, however, with those who were heads of families. A gun was owned by William Foster, and with it, on the 14th of November, near the present Alder Creek Mill, Mr. Eddy succeeded in killing a bear. This event inspired many hearts with courage; but, alas! it was short-lived. No other game could be found except two or three wild ducks. What were these among eighty-one people! Mr. F. W. Graves was a native of Vermont, and his boyhood days had been spent in sight of the Green Mountains. Somewhat accustomed to snow, and to pioneer customs, Mr. Graves was the only member of the party who understood how to construct snow-shoes. The unsuccessful attempt made by the first party proved that no human being could walk upon the loose snow without some artificial assistance. By carefully sawing the ox-bows into strips, so as to preserve their curved form, Mr. Graves, by means of rawhide thongs, prepared very serviceable snow-shoes. Fourteen pair of shoes were made in this manner. It was certain death for all to remain in camp, and yet the first attempt had shown that it was almost equally certain death to attempt to reach the settlements. There was not food for all, and yet the ones who undertook to cross the mountains were undoubtedly sacrificing their lives for those who remained in camp. If some should go, those who were left behind might be able to preserve life until Spring, or until relief came. The stoutest hearts quailed before the thought of battling with the deep drifts, the storms, and the unknown dangers which lurked on the summits. The bravest shuddered at the idea of leaving the cabins and venturing out into the drear and dismal wilderness of snow. Yet they could count upon their fingers the days that would elapse before the provisions would be exhausted, and starvation would ensue, if none left the camps.

Day after day, with aching hearts and throbbing brows, the poor imprisoned wretches gazed into each other's faces in blank despair. Who should be sacrificed? Who would go out and seek a grave 'neath the crashing avalanche, the treacherous drifts, or in the dreary famished wilderness, that those left behind might live? Who would be the forlorn hope of the perishing emigrants?

Once, Messrs. Patrick Breen, Patrick Dolan, Lewis Keseberg, and W. H. Eddy, are said to have attempted to reach the summit. On another occasion these same parties, with Mrs. Reed and family, Mr. Stanton and the two Indians, made an unsuccessful attempt. Still another time, a large party, among whom were Mrs. Murphy and the older members of her family, made the effort, and even succeeded in reaching Summit Valley. But all these parties were forced to return to the cabins, and each failure confirmed the belief that no living being could cross the mountains. In this manner time dragged wearily along until the 10th, or as some say, the 16th of December. The mere matter of the date is of trifling importance. At all events a forlorn hope was organized. Seventeen names were enrolled as volunteers. Of these, Charles Burger went only a short distance, turning back weary and exhausted. Wm. G. Murphy, who is described as a most brave and resolute boy of eleven years of age, accompanied the party as far as the head of Donner Lake. He and his brother Lemuel were without snow-shoes. It was expected they would step in the beaten tracks of those who had shoes, but this was soon proven to be utterly impracticable. The party made snow-shoes for Lemuel on the first night, out of the *aparajos* which had been brought by Stanton from Sutter's Fort. Wm. G. Murphy saved his life by returning to the cabins. No human being could have endured the trip without snow-shoes. Fifteen remained in the party, and these pressed forward without so much as daring to look back to the dear ones whose lives depended upon this terrible venture. Without forgetting William G. Murphy and Charles Burger, who started with this little band, the first party who crossed the Sierras will in future be termed the fifteen. Who composed this party? Mothers, whose babes would starve unless the mothers went; fathers whose wives and children would perish if the fathers did not go; children, whose aged parents could not survive unless the children, by leaving, increased the parents' share of food. Of each was the forlorn hope.

It was time for some one to leave the cabins. During the days that had elapsed, no word had been received from the Donner brothers at Alder Creek, nor from the emigrants who camped with them. Alder Creek is a branch of Prosser Creek, and the Donners encamped on the former stream a short distance above the junction.

On the 9th of December, Milton Elliott and Noah James started back to learn some tidings of these people. Soon after they left the camps at the Lake, a terrific storm came down from the mountains, and as nothing had been heard from them, it was considered certain they had perished.

About this time, starvation and exposure had so preyed upon one of the company, Augustus Spitzer, that one day he came reeling and staggering into the Breen cabin and fell prostrate and helpless upon the floor. Poor fellow, he never rallied, although by careful nursing and kindest attentions he lingered along for some weeks. The emigrants were no longer on short allowance, they were actually starving. Oh! the horror! the dread alarm which prevailed among the company! C. T. Stanton, ever brave, courageous, lion-hearted, said, " I will bring help to these famishing people or lay down my life." F. W. Graves, who was one of the noblest men who ever breathed the breath of life, was next to volunteer. Mr. and Mrs. Graves had nine children, the youngest being only nine months old. Generously had they parted with the cattle which they brought to the lake, dividing equally with those families who had no food. Mary. A. Graves and her elder sister, Mrs. Sarah Fosdick, determined to accompany their father, and as will presently be seen, their hearts failed not during trials which crushed strong men. Jay Fosdick resolved to· share with his wife the perils of the way. Mrs. Murphy offered to take care of the infant children of her married daughters, Mrs. Foster and Mrs. Pike, if they would join the party. The dear good mother urged the argument that what the daughters would eat would keep her and the little ones from starving. It was nobly said, yet who can doubt but that, with clearer vision, the mother saw that only by urging them to go, could she save her daughters' lives. With what anguish did Mrs. Harriet F. Pike enroll her name among those of the forlorn hope, and bid good-bye to her little two-year old Naomi and her nursing babe, Catherine. What bitter tears were shed by Mr. and Mrs. Foster, when they kissed their beautiful baby boy farewell. Alas! though they knew it not, it was a long, long farewell. Mrs. Eddy was too feeble to attempt the journey, and the family were so poorly provided with food that Mr. Eddy was compelled to leave her and the two little children in the cabins, and go with the party. Mrs. McCutchen also had an infant babe, and Mrs. Graves employed the same reasoning with her that Mrs. Murphy had so effectively used with Mrs. Pike and Mrs. Foster. That these three young mothers left their infant children, their nursing babes, with others, and started to find relief, is proof stronger than words, of the desperate condition of the starving emigrants. The Mexican, Antoine, the two Indians, Lewis and Salvador, and an Irishman, named Patrick Dolan, completed the fifteen. This Patrick Dolan deserves more than a passing word. He had owned a farm in Keokuk, Iowa, and selling it, had taken as the price, a wagon, four oxen, and two cows. With these he joined the Donner Party, and on reaching the lake had killed his cattle and stored them away with those killed by the Breens. Dolan was a bachelor, and about forty years of age. He was possessed of two or three hundred dollars in coin, but instead of being miserly or selfish, was characterized by generous open-heartedness. "When it became apparent that there was to be suffering and starvation (this quotation is from the manuscript of Hon. James F. Breen), Dolan determined to lighten the burden at the camps, and leave with the party that was to attempt the passage of the summit, so that there should be less to consume the scant supply of provisions. Previous to his departure, he asked my father (Patrick Breen) to attend to the wants of Reed's family, and to give of his (Dolan's) meat to Reed's family as long as possible." Accordingly, Mrs. Reed and her children were taken into Breen's cabin, where, as mentioned above, Dolan's meat was stored. Was ever a more generous act recorded? Patrick Dolan had no relative in the Donner Party, and no friends save those whose friendship had been formed upon the plains. With the cattle which belonged to him he could have selfishly subsisted until relief came, but, whole-souled Irishman that he was, he gave food to the mothers and the children and went out into the waste of snow to perish of starvation! How many who live to-day owe their existence to Patrick Dolan's self-sacrifice! This blue-eyed, brown-haired Irishman, is described as being of a jovial disposition, and inclined to look upon the bright side of things. Remembering how he gave his life for strangers, how readily can we appreciate Mr. Breen's tender tribute: "He was a favorite with children, and would romp and play with a child." As a token of appreciation for his kindness, Mrs. Reed gave Patrick Dolan a gold watch and a Masonic emblem belonging to her husband, bidding him to keep them until he was rewarded for his generosity. The good mother's word had a significance she wot not of. When Mrs. Reed reached Sutter's Fort she found these valuables awaiting her. They had been brought in by Indians. Patrick Dolan had kept them until his death—until the angels came and bore him away to his reward.

This party of fifteen had taken provisions to last only six days. At the end of this time they hoped to reach Bear Valley, so they said, but it is more than probable that they dared not take more food from their dear ones at the cabins. Six days rations! This means enough of the poor shriveled beef to allow each person, three times a day, a piece the size of one's two fingers. With a little coffee and a little loaf sugar, this was all. They had matches, Foster's gun, a hatchet, and each a thin blanket. With this outfit they started to cross the Sierras. No person unaccustomed to snow-shoes can form an idea of the difficulty which is experienced during one's first attempt to walk with them. Their shoes would sink deep into the loose, light snow, and it was with great effort that they made any progress. They had been at Donner Lake from forty-two to forty-six days, and on this first night of their journey had left it four miles behind them. After a dreadful day's work they encamped, in full sight of the lake and of the cabins. This was harder for the aching hearts of the mothers than even the terrible parting from their little ones. To see the smoke of the cabins, to awake from their troubled dreams thinking they heard the cry of their starving babes, to stifle the maternal yearnings which prompted them to turn back and perish with their darlings clasped to their breasts, were trials almost unbearable. The next day they traveled six miles. They crossed the summit, and the camps were no longer visible. They were in the solemn fastnesses of the snow-mantled Sierras. Lonely, desolate, forsaken apparently, by God and man, their situation was painfully, distressingly terrible. The snow was wrapped about cliff and forest and gorge. It varied in depth from twelve to sixty feet.

Mrs. M. A. Clarke (Mary Graves) now of White River, Tulare County, speaking of this second day, says : " We had a very slavish day's travel, climbing the divide. Nothing of interest occurred until reaching the summit. The scenery was too grand for me to pass without notice, the changes being so great ; walking now on loose snow, and now stepping on a hard, slick rock a number of hundred yards in length. Being a little in the rear of the party, I had a chance to observe the company ahead, trudging along with packs on their backs. It reminded me of some Norwegian fur company among the icebergs. My shoes were ox-bows split in two, and rawhide strings woven in, something in form of the old-fashioned split-bottomed chairs. Our clothes were of the bloomer costume, and generally were made of flannel. Well do I remember a remark one of the company made here, that we were about as near Heaven as we could get. We camped a little on the west side of the summit the second night."

Here they gathered a few boughs, kindled a fire upon the surface of the snow, boiled their coffee and ate their pitiful allowance of beef. Then wrapping their toil-worn bodies in their blankets, lay down upon the snow. As W. C. Graves remarks, it was a bed that

4

was soft, and white, and beautiful—and yet it was a terrible bed, a
bed of death. The third day they walked five miles. Starting
almost at dawn, they struggled wearily through the deep drifts,
and when the night shadows crept over crag and pine and
mountain vale, they were but five miles on their journey. They did
not speak during this day, except when speech was absolutely
necessary. All traveled silently, and with downcast eyes. . The task
was beginning to tell upon the frames of even the strongest and
most resolute. The hunger that continually gnawed at their vitals,
the excessive labor of moving the heavy, clumsy snow-shoes through
the soft, yielding snow, was too much for human endurance. They
could no longer keep together and aid each other with words of
hope. They struggled along, sometimes at great distances from
each other. The fatigue and dazzling sunlight rendered some of
them snow-blind. Among them was the noble-hearted Stanton.
On this third day he was too blind and weak to keep up with the
rest, and staggered into the camp long after the others had finished
their pitiful supper. Poor, brave, generous Stanton. He said little,
but in his inner heart he knew that the end of his journey was
almost at hand.

Who was this heroic being who left the beautiful valleys of the
Sacramento to die for strangers? See him wearily toiling onward
during the long hours of the fourth day. The agony and blindness
of his eyes wring no cry from his lips, no murmur, no word of
complaint. With patient courage and heroic fortitude he strives to
keep pace with his companions, but finds it impossible. Early in
the morning he drops to the rear, and is soon lost to sight. At
night he drags his weary limbs into camp long after his comrades
are sleeping 'neath the silent stars. It must be remembered that
they had been accustomed to short allowance of food for months,
while he had been used to having an abundance. Their bodies had
been schooled to endure famine, privations and long, weary walks.
For many days before reaching the mountains, they had been used
to walking day after day in order to lighten the burdens of the
perishing oxen. Fatigues which exhausted them crushed Stanton.

The weather was clear and pleasant, but the glare of the sun during the day had been like molten fire to their aching eyes.

On the morning of the fifth day Stanton was sitting smoking by the smouldering fire when the company resumed its journey. Mary Graves, who had a tender heart for the suffering of others, went kindly up to him, and asked him if he were coming. "Yes," he replied, "I am coming soon." Was he answering her or the unseen spirits that even then were beckoning him to the unknown world. "Yes, I am coming soon!" These were his last words. His companions were too near death's door to return when they found he came not, and so he perished. He had begged them piteously to lead him, during the first days of his blindness, but seeming to realize that they were unable to render assistance, he ceased to importune, and heroically met his fate. He did not blame his comrades. They were weak, exhausted and ready to die of starvation. With food nearly gone, strength failing, hope lost, and nothing left but the last, blind, clinging instinct of life, it was impossible that the perishing company should have aided the perishing Stanton. He was a hero of the highest, noblest, grandest stamp. No words can ever express a fitting tribute to his memory. He gave his life for strangers who had not the slightest claim to the sacrifice. He left the valleys where friends, happiness and abundance prevailed, to perish amidst chilling snow-drifts—famished and abandoned. The act of returning to save the starving emigrants is as full of heroic grandeur as his death is replete with mournful desolation.

In May, 1847, W. C. Graves, in company with a relief party, found the remains of C. T. Stanton near the spot were he had been left by his companions. The wild animals had partially devoured his body, but the remains were easily identified by means of his clothing and pistols.

The following sketch of this hero is kindly furnished by his brother, Sidney Stanton, of Cazenovia, New York:

"Charles Tyler Stanton was born at Pompey, Onondaga County, New York, March 11th, 1811. He was five feet five inches in height. He had brown eyes and brown hair. He possessed a robust constitution, and although rather slender during his youth, at the age of fifteen he became strong and hearty, and could endure as great hardships as any of his brothers. He had five brothers and four sisters, and was the seventh child. His grand parents on his father's side were well off at the close of the Revolutionary War, but sold their large farms and took Continental money in payment. Soon afterward this money became worthless, and they lost all. They were at the time living in Berkshire, Massachusetts, but soon after removed west to the county were C. T. Stanton was born. There were in his father's family fourteen children—seven sons and seven daughters."

In his younger days Stanton was engaged as a clerk in a store. He was honest, industrious and greatly beloved by those with whom he came in contact. His early education was limited, but during his employment as clerk he used every possible endeavor to improve his mind. During his journey across the plains he was regarded as somewhat of a savant, on account of his knowledge of botany, geology and other branches of natural science. His disposition was generous to a fault. He never was happier than when bestowing assistance upon needy friends. His widowed mother,' for whom he entertained the most devoted affection, was kindly cared for by him until her death in 1835. After this sad event he removed to Chicago. At Chicago he made money rapidly for a time, and his hand was ever ready to give aid to those about him. Charity and heroic self-sacrifice appear to have been his predominant characteristics. They stand out in bold relief, not only in his early history, but during his connection with the Donner Party. While in the mountains he had no money to give, but instead he gave his strength, his energy, his love, his all, his very life, for his companions.

That he had a premonition of the gloomy fate which overtook him in the Sierras, is indicated by the following incident: When he set out from Sutter's Fort to return to the Donner train with provisions, he left a vest with Captain Sutter. In one of the pockets of this vest was subsequently found a package directed to the Captain with the following memorandum: "Captain Sutter will send the within, in the event of my death, to Sidney Stanton, Syracuse, New York." The package contained a diamond breastpin. Mr. Sidney Stanton writes as follows concerning this keepsake :

"I will give you a short history or account of the pin which was left for me at Sutter's Fort, which Mr. McKinstry forwarded to me. This was an event so peculiar at the time. He visited me here at Syracuse, while he was prospering in Chicago. He was on his way to New York, and wanted a sum of money which I advanced. Before leaving he fastened this pin on the dress of my wife, re-marking that she must consider it as a present from him. Nothing more was thought of this event 'until he again wanted money. Misfortune had overtaken him, and this event gave him much pain, not so much on his own account as because he could not relieve the distress of dear friends when asked for aid. I sent him a little more money ; I had not much to spare, and in talking the matter over with my wife, she asked, "Why not send him the pin? it is valuable, and in time of need he might dispose of it for his comfort." In saying this she took the ground that it was left with her as a pledge, not as a gift. I therefore handed it to my sister to send it to him for this purpose. But it appears by his keeping it and sending it back in the way he did that he did consider it a gift, and hence he would not and did not dispose of it for necessary things for his own comfort. This pin was the only thing of value which he had at the time of his death."

Stanton was an excellent writer. His descriptions of his travels from Chicago to the South Pass would make a good sized and a very interesting book. His last composition is given below. It is an appropriate ending to this brief outline of the history of one who should be regarded as one of the noblest of California's pioneer heroes :

"TO MY MOTHER IN HEAVEN.

"Oh! how that word my soul inspires
With holy, fond and pure desires !
Maternal love, how bright the flame !
For wealth of worlds I'd not profane
Nor idly breathe thy sacred name,
My mother.

"Thy sainted spirit dwells on high.
How oft I weep, how oft I sigh
    Whene'er I think of bygone time.
    Thy smile of love, which once was mine,
    That look so heavenly and divine,
        My mother.

"Thy warning voice in prayers of love
Ascending to the throne above
    With tones of eloquence so rife,
    Hath turned my thoughts from worldly strife,
    And cheered me through my wayward life,
        My mother.

"When death shall close my sad career,
And I before my God appear—
    There to receive His last decree—
    My only prayer there will be
    Forever to remain with thee,
        My mother."

CHAPTER VII.

LET no one censure Stanton's companions for abandoning
their brave comrade. In less than twenty-four hours all
were without food, unless, indeed, it was Mr. Eddy, who
in his narration published by Judge Thornton, states that on
the day of Stanton's death he found half a pound of bear's
meat, which had been secreted in a little bag by his wife.
Attached to this meat was a paper upon which his wife had written
in pencil a note signed "Your own dear Eleanor." Mr. Eddy had
not discovered this meat until the sorest hour of need, and the hope
expressed in Mrs. Eddy's note, that it would be the means of saving
his life, was literally fulfilled. There is something extremely touching in the thought that this devoted wife, who was starving to death
in the cabins, saved her husband's life by clandestinely concealing
about his person a portion of the food which should have sustained
herself and her infant children.

In the account given by Mary Graves is mentioned the following
incident in the fourth day's travel: "Observing by the way a deep
gorge at the right, having the appearance of being full of smoke, I
wanted very much to go to it, but the Indians said no, that was not

the way. I prevailed on the men to fire the gun, but there was no answer. Every time we neared the gorge I would halloo at the top of my voice, but we received no answer."

On this day the horror of the situation was increased by the commencement of a snow-storm. As the flakes fell thick and fast the party sat down in the snow utterly discouraged and heartsick.

Mary Graves says: "What to do we did not know. We held a consultation, whether to go ahead without provisions, or go back to the cabins, where we must undoubtedly starve. Some of those who had children and families wished to go back, but the two Indians said they would go on to Captain Sutter's. I told them I would go too, for to go back and hear the cries of hunger from my little brothers and sisters was more than I could stand. I would go as far as I could, let the consequences be what they might."

There, in the deep, pitiless storm, surrounded on all sides by desolate wastes of snow, the idea was first advanced that life might be sustained if some one were to perish. Since leaving the cabins they had at no time allowed themselves more than one ounce of meat per meal, and for two entire days they had not tasted food. The terrible pangs of hunger must be speedily allayed or death was inevitable. Some one proposed that lots be cast to see who should die. The terrible proposition met with opposition from Foster and others, but slips of paper were actually prepared by some of the men, and he who drew the longest—the fatal slip—was Patrick Dolan! Who should take Dolan's life? Who was to be the executioner of the man who had so generously given up the food which might have sustained his life and joined the forlorn hope that others might live? With one accord they rose to their feet and staggered forward. As if to banish from their minds the horrid thought of taking Dolan's life, they attempted to pursue their journey.

With the greatest exertion and suffering they managed to crawl and stagger and flounder along until they attained a distance of two or three miles. Here they camped, and passed a most wretched, desolate night. The morning dawned dreary, rainy and discouraging. The little party set out as usual, but were too weak and lifeless to travel. The soft snow clung to their feet in heavy lumps, like snow-balls. Instead of making a fire in a new place, Mary Graves says they crawled back to the camp-fire of the night previous. Here they remained until night came on—a night full of horrors. The wind howled through the shrieking forests like troops of demons. The rain had continued all day, but finally changed to snow and sleet, which cut their pinched faces, and made them shiver with cold. All the forces of nature seemed to combine for their destruction. At one time during the night, in attempting to kindle a fire the ax or hatchet which they had carried was lost in the loose snow.

A huge fire was kindled at last, with the greatest difficulty, and in order to obtain more warmth all assisted in piling fuel upon the flames. Along in the night, Mrs. Foster thinks it was near midnight, the heat of the flames and the dropping coals and embers thawed the snow underneath the fire until a deep well-like cavity was formed about the fire. Suddenly, as if to intensify the dreadful horrors of the situation, the bottom of this well gave way and the fire disappeared. The camp and the fire had been built over a stream of water, and the fire had melted through the overlying snow until it had fallen into the stream. Those who peered over the brink of the dark opening about which they were gathered, could hear far down in the gloom, during the lull of the storm, the sound of running waters.

If there is anything lacking in this picture of despair, it is furnished in the groans and cries of the shivering, dying outcasts, and the demonical shrieks and ravings of Patrick Dolan, who was in the delirium which precedes death. It was not necessary that life should be taken by the members of the company. Death was busily at work, and before the wild Winter night was ended, his ghastly victims were deaf to wind or storm.

When the fire disappeared it became apparent that the entire forlorn hope would perish before morning if exposed to the cold and storm. W. H. Eddy says the wind increased until it was a perfect tornado. About midnight, Antoine, overcome by starvation, fatigue and the bitter cold, ceased to breathe. Mr. F. W. Graves was dying. There was a point beyond which an iron nerve and a powerful constitution were unable to sustain a man. This point had been reached, and Mr. Graves was fast passing away. He was conscious, and calling his weeping, grief-stricken daughters to his side, exhorted them to use every means in their power to prolong their lives. He reminded them of their mother, of their little brothers and sisters in the cabin on the lake. He reminded Mrs. Pike of her poor babies. Unless these daughters succeeded in reaching Sutter's Fort, and were able to send back relief, all at the lake must certainly die. Instances had been cited in history where, under less provocation, human flesh had been eaten, yet Mr. Graves well knew that his daughters had said they would never touch the loathsome food.

Was there not something noble and grand in the dying advice of this father? Was he not heroic when he counseled that all false delicacy be laid aside and that his body be sacrificed to support those that were to relieve his wife and children?

Earnestly pleading that these afflicted children rise superior to their prejudices and natural instincts—Franklin Ward Graves died. A sublimer death seldom is witnessed. In the solemn darkness, in the tempestuous storm, on the deep frozen snow-drifts, overcome by pain and exposure, with the pangs of famine gnawing away his life, this unselfish father, with his latest breath urged that his flesh be used to prolong the lives of his companions. Truly, a soul that could prompt such utterances had no need, after death, for its mortal tenement—it had a better dwelling-place on high.

With two of their little number in the icy embraces of death, some plan to obtain warmth for the living was immediately necessary. W. H. Eddy proposed a frontiersman's method. It was for all to huddle closely together in a circle, lie down on a blanket with their heads outward, and be covered with a second blanket. Mr. Eddy arranged his companions, spread the blanket over them, and creeping under the coverlid, completed the circle. The wind swept the drifting snow in dense clouds over their heads. The chilling air, already white with falling snowflakes, became dense with the drifting masses. In a little while the devoted band were completely hidden from wind, or storm, or piercing cold, by a deep covering of snow. The warmth of their bodies, confined between the blankets, under the depth of snow, soon rendered them comfortably warm. Their only precaution now was to keep from being buried alive. Occasionally some member of the party would shake the rapidly accumulating snow from off their coverlid.

They no longer were in danger of freezing. But while the elements were vainly waging fierce war above their heads, hunger was rapidly sapping the fountains of life, and claiming them for its victims. When, for a moment, sleep would steal away their reason, in famished dreams they would seize with their teeth the hand or arm of a companion. The delirium of death had attacked one or two, and the pitiful wails and cries of these death-stricken maniacs were heartrending. The dead, the dying, the situation, were enough to drive one crazy.

The next day was ushered in by one of the most furious storms ever witnessed in the Sierras. All the day long, drifts and the fast falling snow circled above them under the force of the fierce gale. The air was a frozen fog of swift darting ice-lances. The fine particles of snow and sleet, hurled by maddened storm-fiends, would cut and sting so that one's eyes could not be opened in the storm, and the rushing gale would hurl one prostrate on the snow. Once or twice the demented Dolan escaped from his companions and disappeared in the blinding storm. Each time he returned or was caught and dragged 'neath the covering, but the fatal exposure chilled the little life remaining in his pulses. During the afternoon he ceased to shriek, or struggle, or moan. Patrick Dolan, the warm-hearted Irishman, was starved to death.

Mr. Eddy states, in Thornton's work, that they entered this Camp of Death, Friday, December 25th, Christmas. According to his version, they started from the cabins on the 16th day of December, with scanty rations for six days. On the 22d, they consumed the last morsel of their provisions. Not until Sunday noon, Decem-

ber 27th, did the storm break away. They had been over four days
without food, and two days and a half without fire. They were
almost dead.

Is there a mind so narrow, so uncharitable, that it can censure
these poor dying people for the acts of this terrible day? With
their loved ones perishing at Donner Lake, with the horror of a
lingering death staring them in the face, can the most unfeeling
heart condemn them?

Emerging from the dreary prison-house, they attempted to kindle
a fire. Their matches were wet and useless. Their flint-lock gun
would give forth a spark, but without some dry material that would
readily ignite, it was of no avail.

On this morning of the 27th Eddy says that he blew up a powder-
horn in an effort to strike fire under the blankets. His face and
hands were much burned. Mrs. McCutchen and Mrs. Foster were
also burned, but not seriously. For some time all efforts to obtain
a fire proved fruitless. Their garments were drenched by the storm.
Mrs. Pike had a mantle that was lined with cotton. The lining of
this was cut open, and the dryest portion of the cotton was exposed
to the sun's rays, in the hope that it could be made to catch the
spark from the flint. At last they were successful. A fire was kindled in a dead tree, and the flames soon leaped up to the loftiest
branches. The famished, shivering wretches gathered round the
burning tree. So weak and lifeless were they, that when the great
pine limbs burned off and fell crashing about them, neither man nor
woman moved or attempted to escape the threatening danger. All
felt that sudden death would be welcome. They were stunned and
horrified by the dreadful alternative which it was evident they must
accept.

The men finally mustered up courage to approach the dead.
With averted eyes and trembling hand, pieces of flesh were severed
from the inanimate forms and laid upon the coals. It was the very
refinement of torture to taste such food, yet those who tasted lived.
One could not eat. Lemuel Murphy was past relief. A boy about
thirteen years old, Lemuel was dearly loved by his sisters, and, full

of courage, had endeavored to accompany them on the fearful journey. He was feeble when he started from the cabins, and the overwhelming sufferings of the fatal trip had destroyed his remaining strength. Starvation is agony during the first three days, apathy and inanition during the fourth and perhaps the fifth, and delirium from that time until the struggle ceases. When the delirium commences, hope ends. Lemuel was delirious Sunday morning, and when food was placed to his lips he either could not eat or was too near death to revive. All day Mrs. Foster held her brother's head in her lap, and by every means in her power sought to soothe his death agonies. The sunlight faded from the surrounding summits. Darkness slowly emerged from the canyons and enfolded forest and hill-slope in her silent embrace. The glittering stars appeared in the heavens, and the bright, full moon rose over the eastern mountain crests. The silence, the profound solitude, the ever-present wastes of snow, the weird moonlight, and above all the hollow moans of the dying boy in her lap, rendered this night the most impressive in the life of Mrs. Foster. She says she never beholds a bright moonlight without recurring with a shudder to this night on the Sierras. At two o'clock in the morning Lemuel Murphy ceased to breathe. The warm tears and kisses of the afflicted sisters were showered upon lips that would never more quiver with pain.

Until December 29th they remained at the "Camp of Death." Would you know more of the shuddering details? Does the truth require the narration of the sickening minutiæ of the terrible transactions of these days? Human beings were never called upon to undergo more trying ordeals. Dividing into groups, the members of each family were spared the pain of touching their own kindred. Days and perhaps weeks of starvation were awaiting them in the future, and they dare not neglect to provide as best they might. Each of the four bodies was divested of its flesh, and the flesh was dried. Although no person partook of kindred flesh, sights were often witnessed that were blood curdling. Mrs. Foster, as we have seen, fairly worshipped her brother Lemuel. Has human pen power to express the shock of horror this sister received when she saw her

brother's heart thrust through with a stick, and broiling upon the
coals? No man can record or read such an occurrence without a
cry of agony! What then did she endure who saw this cruel sight?

These are facts. They are given just as they came from the lips
of Mrs. Foster, a noble woman, who would have died of horror and
a broken heart but for her starving babe, her mother, and her little
brothers and sisters who were at Donner Lake. Mary Graves cor-
roborates Mrs. Foster, and W. H. Eddy gave a similar version to
Judge Thornton.

The Indian guides, Lewis and Salvador, would not eat this revolting food. They built a fire away from the company, and with true
Indian stoicism endured the agonies of starvation without so much as
beholding the occurrences at the other camp-fire.

Starved bodies possess little flesh, and starving people could carry
but light burdens through such snow-drifts. On these accounts,
the provision which the Almighty seemed to have provided to save
their lives, lasted only until the 31st. On New Year's morning they
ate their mocasins and the strings of their snow-shoes. On the night
before, Lewis and Salvador caught the sound of ominous words, or
perceived glances that were filled with dreadful import, and during
the darkness, they fled.

For several days past the party had been lost. The Indians
could not recognize the country when it was hidden from thirty to
fifty feet in snow. Blindly struggling forward, they gradually separated into three parties. On the 4th, W. H. Eddy and Mary Graves
were in advance with the gun. A starved deer crossed their path
and providentially was slain. Drinking its warm blood and feasting
upon its flesh, this couple waited for the arrival of Mr. and Mrs.
Foster, Mrs. McCutchen and Mrs. Pike, who were some distance
behind. Night came and passed and they did not arrive. Indeed,
Foster was dying for lack of nourishment. Behind this party were
Mr. and Mrs. Jay Fosdick. During the night, Mr. Fosdick perished,
and the faithful wife, after remaining with him until morning,
struggled forward and met Mrs. Foster and a companion. Mrs.
Fosdick related the death of her husband, and upon being informed

of Foster's condition, consented that her husband's body be converted into food. It was done. This was the first time that women's hands had used the knife, but by the act a life was saved. Mrs. Fosdick, although dying, would not touch the food, and but for the venison would not have lived to see the setting of the sun. But what was one small deer among so many famished people? Hide, head, feet, entrails, all were eaten. On the 6th, the last morsel was consumed. They were now without hope. Their journey was apparently interminable. Wearied, foot-sore, freezing at night and tortured by hunger during the day, life could not last many hours. Some one must die ; else none could live and reach the long-talked-of relief. Would it be Eddy, whose wife and two children were behind? Would it be Mrs. Pike, who left two babes? Mrs. McCutchen, who left one? Mr. or Mrs. Foster, whose baby boy was at the cabin? Or would it be Mary Graves or Mrs. Fosdick, who had left mother and family? On the night of the 7th, they lay down upon the snow without having tasted a mouthful of food during the day. Continued famine and exhaustion had so weakened their frames that they could not survive another day. Yet, on the morning of the 7th, they arose and staggered onward. Soon they halted and gathered about some freshly made tracks. Tracks marked by blood! Tracks that they knew had been made by Lewis and Salvador. These Indians had eaten nothing for nine days, and had been without fire or blankets for four days. They could not be far ahead.

CHAPTER VIII.

EANWHILE, how fared it with those left at Donner Lake? About the time the fifteen began their terrible journey, Baylis Williams starved to death. Such food as the rest had was freely given to him, but it did not satisfy the demands of his nature. Quietly, uncomplainingly, he had borne the pangs of famine, and when the company first realized his dreadful condition he was in the delirium which preceded death. Oh! the horror! the dread alarm which this death produced! What words can portray the emotions of the starving emigrants, when they saw one of their number actually perish of hunger before their eyes! Williams died in the Graves cabin, and was buried near the house by W. C. Graves and John Denton.

All the Donner Party were starving. When the cattle were killed the hides had been spread over the cabins in lieu of shingles. These were now taken down and eaten. All the survivors describe the method of preparing this miserable substitute for food. The narration by Mrs. J. M. Murphy (Virginia E. Reed), of San Jose, is among the most vivid. She says the green rawhides were cut into strips and laid upon the coals, or held in the flames until the hair was completely singed off. Either side of the piece of hide was then scraped with a knife until comparatively clean, and was placed in a kettle and boiled until soft and pulpy. There was no salt, and only a little pepper, and yet this substance was all that was between them and starvation. When cold, the boiled hides and the water in which they were cooked became jellied and exactly resembled glue. The tender stomachs of many of the little children revolted at this disagreeable diet, and the loathing they acquired for the sight of this substance still exists in the minds of some of the survivors. To this day, Thomas K. Reed, of San Jose, who was then a tiny three-year old, cannot endure the sight of calf's-foot jelly, or of similar dishes, because of its resemblance to the loathed food which was all his mother could give him in the cabins at Donner Lake.

William G. Murphy describes how they gathered up the old cast-away bones of the cattle—bones from which all the flesh had been previously picked—and boiled, and boiled, and boiled them until they actually would crumble between the teeth, and were eaten. The little children, playing upon the fire-rug in his mother's cabin, used to cut off little pieces of the rug, toast them crisp upon the coals, and then eat them. In this manner, before any one was fairly aware of the fact, the fire-rug was entirely consumed.

The Donner families, at Prosser Creek, were, if possible, even in a sadder condition. In order to give a glimpse of the suffering endured in these two tents, the following is quoted from a letter written by Mrs. W. A. Babcock (Georgia A. Donner); now residing at Mountain View, Santa Clara County: "The families shared with one another as long as they had anything to share. Each one's portion was very small. The hides were boiled, and the bones were burned brown and eaten. We tried to eat a decayed buffalo robe, but it was too tough, and there was no nourishment in it. Some of the few mice that came into camp were caught and eaten. Some days we could not keep a fire, and many times, during both days and nights, snow was shoveled from off our tent, and from around it, that

5

we might not be buried alive.   Mother remarked one day that it had
been two weeks that our beds and the clothing upon our bodies
had been wet.   Two of my sisters and myself spent some days at
Keseberg's cabin.   The first morning we were there they shoveled
the snow from our bed before we could get up.   Very few can believe it possible for human beings to live and suffer the exposure and
hardships endured there."

Oh ! how long and dreary the days were to the hungry children!
Even their very plays and pastimes were pathetic, because of their
piteous, silent allusion to the pangs of starvation.   Mrs. Frank Lewis
(Patty Reed), of San Jose, relates that the poor little famishing girls
used to fill the pretty porcelain tea-cups with fresh fallen snow,
daintily dip it out with teaspoons and eat it, playing it was custard.

Dear Mrs. Murphy had the most sacred and pitiful charge.   It was
the wee nursing babe, Catherine Pike, whose mother had gone with
the " Forlorn Hope," to try if possible to procure relief.   All there
was to give the tiny sufferer, was a little gruel made from snow water
containing a slight sprinkling of coarse flour.   This flour was simply
ground wheat, unbolted.   Day after day the sweet little darling
would lie helplessly upon its grandmother's lap, and seem with its large
sad eyes to be pleading for nourishment.   Mrs. Murphy carefully
kept the little handful of flour concealed—there was only a handful
at the very beginning—lest some of the starving children might get
possession of the treasure.   Each day she gave Catherine a few teaspoonfuls of the gruel.   Strangely enough, this poor little martyr did
not often cry with hunger, but with tremulous, quivering mouth, and
a low subdued sob or moan, would appear to be begging for something to eat.   The poor dumb lips, if gifted with speech, could not
have uttered a prayer half so eloquent, so touching.   Could the
mother, Mrs. Pike, have been present, it would have broken her
heart to see her patient babe dying slowly, little by little.   Starvation
had dried the maternal breasts long before Mrs. Pike went away, so
that no one can censure her for leaving her baby.   She could only
have done as Mrs. Murphy did, give it the plain coarse gruel, and
watch it die day by day upon her lap.

Up to this time but little has been said of Patrick Breen. He was an invalid during the Winter of 1846 and '47. A man of more than ordinary intelligence, a devout Catholic, a faithful and devoted father, his life furnishes a rare type of the pioneer Californian. To Mr. Breen we are indebted for the most faithful and authentic record of the days spent at the cabins. This record is in the form of a diary, in which the events of the day were noted in the order of their occurrence. Lewis Keseberg kept a similar diary, but it was subsequently accidentally destroyed. Mrs. Tamsen Donner kept a journal, but this with her paintings and botanical collections disappeared at the fatal tent on Alder Creek. Mr. Breen's diary alone was preserved. He gave it into Col. McKinstry's possession in the Spring of 1847, and on the fourth of September of that year it was published in the Nashville (Tenn.) Whig. A copy of the Whig of that date is furnished by Wm. G. Murphy, of Marysville. Other papers have published garbled extracts from this diary, but none have been reliable. The future history of the events which transpired at the cabins will be narrated in connection with this diary.

It must be remembered that the lake had always been known as "Truckee Lake," it having been named after an old Indian guide who had rendered much assistance to the Schallenberger party in 1844.

The diary commences as follows :

"TRUCKEY'S LAKE, November 20th, 1846.

"Came to this place on the 31st of last month; went into the pass; the snow so deep we were unable to find the road, and when within three miles from the summit turned back to this shanty on Truckey's Lake; Stanton came up one day after we arrived here; we again took our teams and wagons and made another unsuccessful attempt to cross in company with Stanton; we returned to this shanty; it continued to snow all the time. We now have killed most part of our cattle, having to remain here until next Spring, and live on lean beef, without bread or salt. It snowed during the space of eight days, with little intermission after our arrival, though now clear and pleasant, freezing at night; the snow nearly gone from the valleys.

"November 21. Fine morning; wind northwest; twenty-two of our company about starting to cross the mountains this day, including Stanton and his Indians.

"Nov. 22. Froze last night; fine and clear to-day; no account from those on the mountains.

"Nov. 23. Same weather; wind west; the expedition across the mountains returned after an unsuccessful attempt.

"Nov. 25. Cloudy; looks like the eve of a snow-storm; our mountaineers are to make another trial to-morrow if fair; froze hard last night.

"Nov. 26. Began to snow last evening; now rains or sleets; the party do not start to-day.

"Nov. 27. Still snowing; now about three feet deep; wind west; killed my last oxen to-day; gave another yoke to Foster; wood hard to be got.

"Nov. 30. Snowing fast; looks as likely to continue as when it commenced; no living thing without wings can get about.

"Dec. 1. Still snowing; wind west; snow about six or seven and a half feet deep; very difficult to get wood, and we are completely housed up; our cattle all killed, but two or three, and these with the horses and Stanton's mules all supposed to be lost in the snow; no hopes of finding them alive.

"Dec. 3. Ceases snowing; cloudy all day; warm enough to thaw.

"Dec. 5. Beautiful sunshine; thawing a little; looks delightful after the long storm; snow seven or eight feet deep.

"Dec. 6. The morning fine and clear; Stanton and Graves manufacturing snow-shoes for another mountain scrabble; no account of mules.

"Dec. 8. Fine weather; froze hard last night; wind southwest; hard work to find wood sufficient to keep us warm or cook our beef.

"Dec. 9. Commenced snowing about eleven o'clock; wind northwest; took in Spitzer yesterday, so weak that he cannot rise without help; caused by starvation. Some have a scanty supply of beef;

Stanton trying to get some for himself and Indians; not likely to get much.

"Dec. 10. Snowed fast all night, with heavy squalls of wind; continues to snow; now about seven feet in depth.

"Dec. 14. Snows faster than any previous day; Stanton and Graves, with several others, making preparations to cross the mountains on snow-shoes; snow eight feet on a level.

"Dec. 16. Fair and pleasant; froze hard last night; the company started on snow-shoes to cross the mountains; wind southeast.

"Dec. 17. Pleasant; William Murphy returned from the mountain party last evening; Baylis Williams died night before last; Milton and Noah started for Donner's eight days ago; not returned yet; think they are lost in the snow.

"Dec. 19. Snowed last night; thawing to-day; wind northwest; a little singular for a thaw.

"Dec. 20. Clear and pleasant; Mrs. Reed here; no account from Milton yet. Charles Burger started for Donner's; turned back; unable to proceed; tough times, but not discouraged. Our hope is in God. Amen.

"Dec. 21. Milton got back last night from Donner's camp. Sad news; Jacob Donner, Samuel Shoemaker, Rhinehart and Smith are dead; the rest of them in a low situation; snowed all night, with a strong southwest wind."

Jacob Donner was the first to die at Prosser Creek. He expired while sitting at the table in his tent, with his head bowed upon his hands, as if in deep meditation. The following terse account is from the gifted pen of Mrs. S. O. Houghton (Eliza P. Donner), of San Jose: "Jacob Donner was a slight man, of delicate constitution, and was in poor health when we left Springfield, Illinois. The trials of the journey reduced his strength and exhausted his energy. When we reached the place of encampment in the mountains he was discouraged and gave up in despair. Not even the needs of his family could rouse him to action. He was utterly dejected and made no effort, but tranquilly awaited death."

"Dec. 23. Clear to-day; Milton took some of his meat away; all well at their camp. Began this day to read the 'Thirty Days' Prayers;' Almighty God, grant the requests of unworthy sinners!

"Dec. 24. Rained all night, and still continues; poor prospect for any kind of comfort, spiritual or temporal."

As will be seen by various references throughout this diary, Mr. Breen was a dèvout Catholic. During the darkest hour of trial, the prayers were regularly read. That this might be done during the long weary evenings, as well as by day, pieces of pitch pine were split and laid carefully in one corner of the cabin, which would be lighted at the fire, and would serve as a substitute for candles. Those of the survivors who are living often speak of the times when they held these sticks while Mr. Breen read the prayers. So impressive were these religious observanceš, that one girl, a bright, beautiful child, made a solemn vow that if God would hear these prayers, and deliver her family from the dangers surrounding them, she would become a Catholic. God did save her family, and she kept her vow. She is to-day a fervent Catholic.

" Dec. 25. Began to snow yesterday, snowed all night, and snows yet rapidly; extremely difficult to find wood; uttered our prayers to God this Christmas morning; the prospect is appalling, but we trust in Him."

What a desolate Christmas morning that was for the snow-bound victims. All were starving. Something to eat, something to satisfy the terrible cravings of appetite, was the constant wish of all. Sometimes the wishes were expressed aloud, but more frequently a gloomy silence prevailed. When anything was audibly wished for, it was invariably something whose size was proportional to their hunger. They never wished for a meal, or a mouthful, but for a barrel full, a wagon load, a house full, or a storehouse full.

On Christmas eve the children spoke in low, subdued tones, of the visits Santa Claus used to make them in their beautiful homes, before they started across the plains.   Now they knew that no Santa Claus could find them in the pathless depths of snow.

One family, the Reeds, were in a peculiarly distressing situation. They knew not whether the father was living or dead.   No tidings had reached them since his letters ceased to be found by the way-side.   The meat they had obtained from the Breen and Graves families was now gone, and on Christmas morning their breakfast was a " pot of glue," as the boiled rawhide was termed.   But Mrs. Reed, the dear, tender-hearted mother, had a surprise in store for her children this day.   When the last ox had been purchased, Mrs. Reed had placed the frozen meat in one corner of the cabin, so that pieces could be chipped off with a knife or hatchet.   The tripe, how-ever, she cleaned carefully and hung on the outside of the cabin, on the end of a log, close to the ground.   She knew that the snow would soon conceal this from view.   She also laid away secretly, one teacupful of white beans, about half that quantity of rice, the same measure of dried apples, and a piece of bacon two inches square. She knew that if Christmas found them alive, they would be in a terribly destitute condition.   She therefore resolved to lay these arti-cles away, and give them to her starving children for a Christmas dinner.   This was done.   The joy and gladness of these poor little children knew no bounds when they saw the treasures unearthed and cooking on the fire.   They were, just this one meal, to have all they could eat!   They laughed, and danced, and cried by turns.   They eagerly watched the dinner as it boiled.   The pork and tripe had been cut in dice-like pieces.   Occasionally one of these pieces would boil up to the surface of the water for an instant, then a bean would take a peep at them from the boiling kettle, then a piece of apple, or a grain of rice.   The appearance of each tiny bit was hailed by the children with shouts of glee.   The mother, whose eyes were brimming with tears, watched her famished darlings with emotions that can be imagined.   It seemed too sad that innocent children should be brought to such destitution that the very sight of food should so affect them!   When the dinner was prepared, the mother's constant injunction was, " Children, eat slowly, there is plenty for all." When they thought of the starvation of to-morrow, they could not repress a shade of sadness, and when the name of Papa was mentioned all burst into tears. Dear, brave Papa! Was he struggling to relieve his starving family, or lying stark and dead 'neath the snows of the Sierras? This question was constantly uppermost in the mother's mind.

"Dec. 27. Cleared off yesterday, and continues clear; snow nine feet deep; wood growing scarce; a tree when felled sinks into the snow, and is hard to be got at.

"Dec. 30. Fine clear morning; froze hard last night. Charles Burger died last evening about 10 o'clock.

"Dec. 31. Last of the year. May we, with the help of God, spend the coming year better than we have the past, which we propose to do if it is the will of the Almighty to deliver us from our present dreadful situation. Amen. Morning fair, but cloudy ; wind east-by-south ; looks like another snow-storm. Snow-storms are dreadful to us. The snow at present is very deep.

"Jan. 1, 1847. We pray the God of Mercy to deliver us from our present calamity, if it be His holy will. Commenced snowing last night, and snows a little yet. Provisions getting very scanty; dug up a hide from under the snow yesterday; have not commenced on it yet.

"Jan. 3. Fair during the day, freezing at night. Mrs. Reed talks of crossing the moutains with her children.

"Jan. 4. Fine morning ; looks like Spring. Mrs. Reed and Virginia, Milton Elliott, and Eliza Williams started a short time ago with the hope of crossing the mountains ; left the children here. It was difficult for Mrs. Reed to part with them."

This expedition was only one of many that the emigrants attempted. The suffering that was endured at these times was indescribable. The broken, volcanic nature of the summits rendered it extremely difficult to keep from getting lost. The white, snowy cliffs were everywhere the same. This party became bewildered and lost near the beautiful Lake Angeline. Had they attempted to proceed, all would undoubtedly have perished.

Within half a mile of the present wagon road from Donner Lake to the Summit are places where rocks and cliffs are mingled in wildest confusion. Even in Summer time it is difficult to find one's way among the broken, distorted mountain tops. In the mighty upheaval which produced the Sierra Nevadas, these vast mounds or mountains of frowning granite were grouped into weird fantastic labyrinths. Time has wrought little effect upon their bold precipitous sides, and made slight impress upon their lofty and almost inaccessible crests. Between these fragmentary mountains, in shapely symmetrical bowls which have been delved by the fingers of the water nymphs and Undines, lie beautiful lakelets. Angeline is but one of a dozen which sparkle like a chain of gems between Donner Lake and the snowy overhanging peaks of Mount Stanford. The clefts and fissures of the towering granite cliffs are filled, in Summer, with dainty ferns, clinging mosses, and the loveliest of mountain wild flowers, and the rims of the lakelets are bordered with grasses, shrubbery, and a wealth of wild blossoms. But in Winter this region exhibits the very grandeur of desolation. No verdure is visible save the dwarfed and shattered pines whose crushed branches mark the path of the rushing avalanches. The furious winds in their wild sport toss and tumble the snow-drifts here and there, baring the sterile peaks, and heaping the white masses a hundred feet deep into chasm and gorge. The pure, clear lakes, as if in very fear, hide their faces from the turbulent elements in mantles of ice. The sun is darkened by dense clouds, and the icy, shivering, shrieking storm fiends hold undisturbed their ghastly revels. On every side are lofty battlements of rock, whose trembling burden of snow seems ever ready to slide from its glassy foundations of ice, and entomb the bewildered traveler.

Into this interminable maze of rocks and cliffs and frozen lakelets, the little party wandered. Elliott had a compass, but it soon proved worthless, and only added to their perplexed and uncertain state of mind. They were out five days. Virginia's feet became so badly frozen that she could not walk. This occurrence saved the party.

Reluctantly they turned back toward the cabins, convinced that it was madness to attempt to go forward. They reached shelter just as one of the most terrible storms of all that dreadful Winter broke over their heads. Had they delayed their return a few hours, the path they made in ascending the mountains would have been concealed, and death would have been certain.

"Jan. 6. Eliza came back yesterday evening from the mountains, unable to proceed; the others kept ahead.

"Jan. 8. Mrs. Reed and the others came back; could not find their way on the other side of the mountains. They have nothing but hides to live on.

"Jan. 10. Began to snow last night; still continues; wind west-northwest.

"Jan. 13. Snowing fast; snow higher than the shanty; it must be thirteen feet deep. Cannot get wood this morning; it is a dreadful sight for us to look upon."

One of the stumps near the Graves-Reed cabin, cut while the snow was at its deepest, was found, by actual measurement, to be twenty-two feet in height. Part of this stump is standing to-day.

"Jan. 14. Cleared off yesterday. The sun, shining brilliantly, renovates our spirits. Praise be to the God of Heaven.

"Jan. 15. Clear to-day again. Mrs. Murphy blind; Landrum not able to get wood; has but one ax between him and Keseberg. It looks like another storm; expecting some account from Sutter's soon.

"Jan. 17. Eliza Williams came here this morning; Landrum crazy last night; provisions scarce; hides our main subsistence. May the Almighty send us help.

"Jan. 21. Fine morning; John Baptiste and Mr. Denton came this morning with Eliza; she will not eat hides. Mrs. ——— sent her back to live or die on them."

The blanks which occasionally occur were in the original diary. The delicacy which prompted Patrick Breen to omit these names cannot fail to be appreciated. What if there was sometimes a shade of selfishness, or an act of harshness? What if some families had more than their destitute neighbors? The best provided had little. All were in reality strangely generous. All divided with their afflicted companions. The Reeds had almost nothing to eat when they arrived at the cabins, yet this family is the only one which reached the settlements without some one. member having to partake of human flesh.

"Jan. 22. Began to snow after sunrise; likely to continue; wind north.

"Jan. 23. Blew hard and snowed all night; the most severe storm we have experienced this Winter; wind west.

"Jan. 26. Cleared up yesterday; to-day fine and pleasant; wind south; in hopes we are done with snow-storms. Those who went to Sutter's not yet returned; provisions getting scant; people growing weak, living on a small allowance of hides.

"Jan. 27. Commenced snowing yesterday; still continues to-day. Lewis Keseberg, Jr., died three days ago; food growing scarce; don't have fire enough to cook our hides.

"Jan. 30. Fair and pleasant; wind west; thawing in the sun. John and Edward Breen went to Graves' this morning. Mrs. —— seized on Mrs. ——'s goods until they would be paid; they also took the hides which herself and family subsisted upon. She regained two pieces only, the balance they have taken. You may judge from this what our fare is in camp. There is nothing to be had by hunting, yet perhaps there soon will be.

"Jan. 31. The sun does not shine out brilliant this morning; froze hard last night; wind northwest. Landrum Murphy died last night about ten o'clock; Mrs. Reed went to Graves' this morning to look after goods."

Landrum Murphy was a large and somewhat overgrown young man.   The hides and burnt bones did not contain sufficient nourishment to keep him alive.   For some hours before he died he lay in a semi-delirious state, breathing heavily and seemingly in little or no pain.   Mrs. Murphy went to the Breen camp and asked Mrs. Breen for a piece of meat to save her starving boy.   Mrs. Breen gave her the meat, but it was too late.   Landrum could not eat.   Finally he sank into a gentle slumber.   His breathing grew less and less distinct, and ere they were fairly aware of it life was extinct.

"Feb. 4.   Snowed hard until twelve o'clock last night; many uneasy for fear we shall all perish with hunger; we have but little meat left, and only three hides; Mrs. Reed has nothing but one hide, and that is on Graves' house; Milton lives there, and likely will keep that.   Eddy's child died last night.

"Feb. 5.   It snowed faster last night and to-day than it has done this Winter before; still continues without intermission; wind southwest.   Murphy's folks and Keseberg say they cannot eat hides.   I wish we had enough of them.   Mrs. Eddy is very weak.

"Feb. 7.   Ceased to snow at last; to-day it is quite pleasant. McCutchen's child died on the second of this month."

This child died and was buried in the Graves cabin.   Mr. W. C. Graves helped dig the grave near one side of the cabin, and laid the little one to rest.   One of the most heart-rending features of this Donner tragedy is the number of infants that suffered.   Mrs. Breen, Pike, Foster, McCutchen, Eddy, Keseberg and Graves each had nursing babes when the fatal camp was pitched at Donner Lake.

"Feb. 8.   Fine clear morning; Spitzer died last night, and we will bury him in the snow; Mrs. Eddy died on the night of the 7th.

"Feb. 9.   Mr. Pike's child all but dead; Milton is at Murphy's, not able to get out of bed; Mrs. Eddy and child were buried to-day; wind southeast.

"Feb. 10. Beautiful morning; thawing in the sun; Milton Elliott died last night at Murphy's cabin, and Mrs. Reed went there this morning to see about his effects. John Denton trying to borrow meat for Graves; had none to give; they had nothing but hides; all are entirely out of meat, but a little we have; our hides are nearly all eat up, but with God's help Spring will soon smile upon us.

"Feb. 12. Warm, thawy morning.

"Feb. 14. Fine morning, but cold. Buried Milton in the snow; John Denton not well.

"Feb. 15. Morning cloudy until nine o'clock, then cleared off warm. Mrs. ———— refused to give Mrs. ———— any hides. Put Sutter's pack-hides on her shanty, and would not let her have them.

"Feb. 16. Commenced to rain last evening, and turned to snow during the night, and continued until morning; weather changeable, sunshine and then light showers of hail, and wind at times. We all feel unwell. The snow is not getting much less at present."

CHAPTER IX.

The Last Resort—Two Reports of a Gun—Weary Traveling—The Snow Bridges
—Human Tracks!—An Indian Rancherie—Acorn Bread—Starving Five
Times!—A Thirty two Days' Journey—Organizing the First Relief Party
—Alcalde Sinclair's Address—Captain R. P. Tucker's Companions.

IT is recorded of Lewis and Salvador that they came willingly
to the relief of the emigrants. Two of Sutter's best trained
vaqueros, faithful, honest, reliable, they seemed rather proud
when chosen to assist Stanton in driving the mules laden
with provisions for the starving train. Now they were dying!
Horrified at the sight of human beings eating the flesh of their
comrades, they withdrew from the whites at the "Camp of Death."
After that they always camped apart, but continued to act as guides
until they became certain that their own lives were in danger. Then
they fled. Starving, exhausted, with frozen and bleeding feet, the
poor wretches dragged their weary bodies onward until they reached
a little streamlet, and here they lay down to die. Nine days, with
no other food than they could find in the snow, was too much even
for their hardy natures. They were unable to move when the
famished "Seven" passed. Yes, PASSED! for the starving emigrants
went on by the poor fellows, unable to deprive them of the little
spark of life left in their wasted bodies. Traveling was now slow
work for the dying whites. They only went about two hundred
yards. In a few more hours, perhaps that very night, they would die

of starvation. Already the terrible phantasies of delirium were beginning to dance before their sunken eyes. Ere the Indians would
cease breathing some of the Seven would be past relief. There
were two men and five women. William Foster could see that his
wife—the woman who was all the world to him—was fast yielding to
the deadly grasp of the fiends of starvation. For the sake of his life
she had stifled the most sacred instincts of her womanly nature, and
procured him food from Fosdick's body. Should he see her die the
most terrible of deaths without attempting to rescue her ! Reader,
put yourself in this man's place. Brave, generous, heroic, full of
lion-like nobility, William Foster could not stoop to a base action.
Contemplate his position ! Lying there prostrate upon the snow,
was Mrs. Pike, the woman whom, accidentally, he had rendered a
widow. Her babes were dying in the cabins. His own boy was at
the cabins. His comrades, his wife, were in the last stages of starvation. He, also, was dying. Eddy had not nerve enough, the women
could not, and William Foster must—what? Was it murder ? No!
Every law book, every precept of that higher law, self-preservation,
every dictate of right, reason or humanity, demanded the deed. The
Indians were past all hope of aid. They could not lift their heads
from their pillow of snow. It was not simply justifiable—it was
duty; it was a necessity.

He told them, when he got back, that he was compelled to take
their lives. They did not moan or struggle, or appear to regret
that their lingering pain was to cease. The five women and Eddy
heard two reports of a gun.

The "Forlorn Hope" might yet save those who were dying at
Donner Lake.

Even this relief was but temporary. Taking the wasted flesh from
the bones, drying it, and staggering forward, the little band speedily
realized that they were not yet saved. It was food for only a few
days. Then they again felt their strength failing. Once more they
endured the excruciating torments which precede starvation.

In the very complete account of this trip, which is kindly furnished by Mary Graves, are many interesting particulars concerning

the suffering of these days.   "Our only chance for camp-fire for the
night," she says, "was to hunt a dead tree of some description, and
set fire to it.   The hemlock being the best and generally much the
largest timber, it was our custom to select the dryest we could find,
without leaving our course.   When the fire would reach the top of
the tree, the falling limbs would fall all around us, and bury themselves in the snow, but we heeded them not.   Sometimes the falling,
blazing limbs would brush our clothes, but they never hit us; that
would have been too lucky a hit.   We would sit or lie on the snow,
and rest our weary frames.   We would sleep, only to dream of something nice to eat, and awake again to disappointment.   Such was our
sad fate!   Even the reindeer's wretched lot was not worse!   'His
dinner and his bed were snow, and supper he had not.'   Our fare
was the same!   We would strike fire by means of the flint-lock gun
which we had with us.   This had to be carried by turns, as it was
considered the only hope left in case we might find game which we
could kill.   We traveled over a ridge of mountains, and then
descended a deep canyon, where one could scarcely see the bottom.
Down, down we would go, or rather slide, for it is very slavish work
going down hill, and in many cases we were compelled to slide on
our shoes as sleds.   On reaching the bottom, we would plunge into
the snow, so that it was difficult getting out, with the shoes tied to
our feet, our packs lashed to our backs, and ourselves head and
ears under the snow.   But we managed to get out some way, and
one by one reached the bottom of the canyon.   When this was
accomplished, we had to ascend a hill as steep as the one we had
descended.   We would drive the toes of our shoes into the loose snow,
to make a sort of step, and one by one, as if ascending stair-steps,.we
climbed up.   It took us an entire day to reach the top of the mountain.   Each time we attained the summit of a mountain, we hoped we
should be able to see something like a valley, but each time came disappointment, for far ahead was always another and higher mountain.
We found some springs, or as we called them, wells, from five to
twenty feet under ground, as you might say, for they were under the
snow on which we walked.   The water was so warm that it melted

the snow, and from some of these springs were large streams of running water. We crossed numbers of these streams on bridges of snow, which would sometimes form upon a blade of grass hanging over the water; and from so small a foundation would grow a bridge from ten to twenty-five feet high, and from a foot and a half to three feet across the top. It would make you dizzy to look down at the water, and it was with much difficulty we could place our clumsy ox-bow snow-shoes one ahead of the other without falling. Our feet had been frozen and thawed so many times that they were bleeding and sore. When we stopped at night, we would take off our shoes, which by this time were so badly rotted by constant wetting in snow, that there was very little left of them. In the morning we would push our shoes on, bruising and numbing the feet so badly that they would ache and ache with walking and the cold, until night would come again. Oh! the pain! It seemed to make the pangs of hunger more excruciating."

Thus the party traveled on day after day, until absolute starvation again stared them in the face. The snow had gradually grown less deep, until finally it disappeared or lay only in patches. Their strength was well nigh exhausted, when one day Mary Graves says : "Some one called out 'Here are tracks !' Some one asked 'What kind of tracks—human?' 'Yes, human!' Can any one imagine the joy these footprints gave us? We ran as fast as our strength would carry us."

Turning a chapparel point, they came in full view of an Indian rancherie. The uncivilized savages were amazed. Never had they seen such forlorn, wretched, pitiable human beings, as the tattered, disheveled, skeleton creatures who stood stretching out their arms for assistance. At first, they all ran and hid, but soon they returned to the aid of these dying wretches. It is said that the Indian women and children cried, and wailed with grief at the affecting spectacle of starved men and women. Such food as they had was speedily offered. It was bread made of acorns. This was eagerly eaten. It

6

was at least a substitute for food.   Every person in the rancherie,
from the toddling papooses to the aged Chief, endeavored to aid
them.

After what had recently happened could anything be more touching than these acts of kindness of the Indians?

After briefly resting they pressed forward.   The Indians accompanied and even led them, and constantly supplied them with food.
With food?   No, it was not such food as their weakened debilitated
systems craved.   The acorn bread was not sufficient to sustain lives
already so attenuated by repeated starvations.   All that the starved
experience in the way of pain and torture before they die, had been
experienced by these people at least four different times.   To their
horror, they now discovered that despite the acorn bread, they must
die of hunger and exhaustion a fifth and last time.   So sick and
weak did they become, that they were compelled to lie down and
rest every hundred yards.   Finally, after being with the Indians seven
days, they lay down, and felt that they never should have strength to
take another step.   Before them, in all its beauty and loveliness,
spread the broad valley of the Sacramento.   Behind them were the
ever-pleading faces of their starving dear ones.   Yet neither hope nor
affection could give them further strength.   They were dying in full
view of the long desired haven of rest.

One of the number was hardly so near death's door as his companions.   It was W. H. Eddy.   As a last resort their faithful allies,
the Indians, took him upon either side, and fairly carried him along.
His feet moved, but they were frozen, and blistered, and cracked,
and bleeding.   Left alone, he would have fallen helplessly to the
earth.   It was as terrible a journey as ever mortal man performed.
How far he traveled, he knew not.   During the last six miles his
path was marked by blood-stains from his swollen feet.

By making abridgements from valuable manuscript contributed by
George W. Tucker, of Calistoga, this narrative may be appropriately
continued.   Mr. Tucker's father and relatives had reached Johnson's
Ranch on the 25th of October, 1846.   They had been with the
Donner Party until Fort Bridger was reached, and then took the

Fort Hall road.   Their journey had been full of dangers and difficulties, and reaching Johnson's Ranch, the first settlement on the
west side of the Sierras, they determined to remain during the
Winter.

One evening, about the last of January, Mr. Tucker says a man
was seen coming down Bear River, accompanied by an Indian.   His
haggard, forlorn look showed he was in great distress.   When he
reached us he said he was of the Donner Party. ˙ He told briefly
how the train had been caught in the snow east of the mountains,
and was unable to get back or forward.   He told how the fifteen
had started, and that six beside himself were still alive.   That the
six were back in the mountains, almost starved.   R. P. Tucker and
three other men started at once with provisions, the Indian acting
as guide.   They reached them, fifteen miles back, some time during
the night, and brought them in next day.   The names of the seven
were W. H. Eddy, William Foster, Mrs. S. A. C. Foster, Mrs. H. F.
Pike, Mrs. William McCutchen, Mrs. Sarah Fosdick and Mary
Graves.   It had been thirty-two days since they left Donner Lake !

At Johnson's Ranch there were only three or four families of poor
emigrants.   Nothing could be done toward relieving those at Donner
Lake until help could arrive from Sutter's Fort.   A rainy Winter
had flooded Bear River, and rendered the Sacramento plains a vast
quagmire.   Yet one man volunteered to go to Sacramento with the
tale of horror, and get men and provisions.   This man was John
Rhodes.   Lashing two pine logs together with rawhides, and forming
a raft, John Rhodes was ferried over Bear River.   Taking his shoes
in his hands, and rolling his pants up above his knees, he started
on foot through water that frequently was from one to three feet
deep.   Some time during the night he reached the Fort.

A train in the mountains !   Men, women and children starving !
It was enough to make one's blood curdle to think of it !   Captain
Sutter, generous old soul, and Alcalde Sinclair, who lived at Norris'
Ranch, two and a half miles from the Fort, offered provisions, and
five or six men volunteered to carry them over the mountains.   In
about a week, six men, fully provided with supplies, reached John-

son's Ranch.   Meantime the Tuckers and their neighbors had slaughtered five or six fat cattle, and had dried or "jerked" the meat.   The country was scoured for horses and mules, and for saddles and pack-saddles, but at last, in ten or twelve days, they were ready to start.   Alcalde Sinclair had come up from the Fort, and when all were ready to begin their march, he made them a thrilling little address.   They were, he said, starting out upon a hazardous journey.   Nothing could justify them in attempting so perilous an undertaking except the obligations due to their suffering fellow men.   He urged them to do all in their power without sac rificing their lives, to save the perishing emigrants from starvation and death.   He then appointed Reasin P. Tucker, the father of our informant, Captain of the company.   With a pencil he carefully wrote down the name of each man in the relief party.   They were John Rhodes, Daniel Rhodes, Aquilla Glover, R. S. Mootrey, Joseph Foster, Edward Coffeemire, M. D. Ritchie, James Curtis, William H. Eddy, William Coon, R. P. Tucker, George W. Tucker and Adolph Brueheim.   Thus the first relief party started.

CHAPTER X.

A Lost Age in California History—The Change Wrought by the Discovery of
Gold—The Start from Johnson's Ranch—A Bucking Horse—A Night Ride—
Lost in the Mountains—A Terrible Night—A Flooded Camp—Crossing a
Mountain Torrent—Mule Springs—A Crazy Companion—Howlings of Gray
Wolves—A Deer Rendezvous—A Midnight Thief—Frightening Indians.

ALIFORNIA at this time was sparsely settled, and it was a
fearful undertaking to cross the snowy mountains to the
relief of the storm-bound emigrants. A better idea of the
difficulties encountered by the various relief parties cannot
be presented than by quoting from the manuscript of George
W. Tucker. This gentleman was sixteen years old at the
time of the occurrences narrated, and his account is vouched for as
perfectly truthful and reliable. This sketch, like the remainder of
this book, treats of an epoch in California history which has been
almost forgotten. The scene of his adventures is laid in a region
familiar to thousands of miners and early Californians. Along the
route over which he passed with so much difficulty, scores of mining
camps sprung up soon after the discovery of gold, and every flat,
ravine and hill-slope echoed to pick, and shovel, and pan, and to
voices of legions of men. Truly, his narration relates to a lost, an
almost unremembered era in the history of the famous mining coun-
ties, Placer and Nevada. In speaking of the first relief party, he
says:

"We mounted our horses and started. The ground was very soft among the foothills, but we got along very well for two or three miles after leaving Johnson's ranch. Finally, one of our pack-horses broke through the crust, and down he went to his sides in the mud. He floundered and plunged until the pack turned underneath his body. He then came out of the mud, bucking and kicking; and he bucked and kicked, and kicked and bucked, till he cleared himself of the pack, pack-saddle and all, and away he went back to the ranch. We gathered up the pack, put it upon the horse Eddy was riding, and the party traveled on. Eddy and myself were to go back to the ranch, catch the horse, and returning overtake them. We failed to find the horse that day, but the next morning an Indian got on my horse, and, about nine o'clock succeeded in finding the missing animal. My horse, however, was pretty well run down when he got back. Eddy and myself started about ten o'clock. We had to travel in one day what the company had traveled in two days. About the time we started it commenced clouding up, and we saw we were going to have a storm. We went on until about one o'clock, when my horse gave out. It commenced raining and was very cold. Eddy said he would ride on and overtake the company, if possible, and have them stop. He did not overtake them until about dark, after they had camped.

" My horse could only go in a slow walk, so I walked and led him to keep from freezing. The rain continued to increase in volume, and by dark it was coming down in torrents. It was very cold. The little stream began to rise, but I waded through, though sometimes it came up to my armpits. It was very dark, but I kept going on in hopes I would come in sight of the camp-fire. But the darkness increased, and it was very difficult to find the road. I would get down on my knees and feel for the road with my hands. Finally, about nine o'clock, it became so dark that I could not see a tree until I would run against it, and I was almost exhausted dragging my horse after me. I had lost the road several times, but found it by feeling for the wagon-ruts. At last I came to where the road made a short turn around the point of a hill, and I went straight

ahead until I got forty or fifty yards from the road. I crawled
around for some time on my knees, but could not find it. I knew
if the storm was raging in the morning as it was then, if I got very
far from the road, I could not tell which was east, west, north or
south—I might get lost and perish before the storm ceased—so I
concluded to stay right there until morning. I had no blanket and
nothing on me but a very light coat and pair of pants. I tied my
horse to a little pine tree, and sitting down leaned against the tree.
The rain came down in sheets. The wind blew, and the old pine
trees clashed their limbs together. It seemed to me that a second
deluge had come. I would get so cold that I would get up and walk
around for awhile. It seemed to me I should surely freeze. Toward
morning I began to get numb, and felt more comfortable, but that
was the longest and hardest night I ever experienced.

"In the morning, when it became light enough so that I could
see two or three rods, I got up, but my legs were so numb that I
could not walk. I rolled around until I got up a circulation, and
could stand on my feet. Leaving my horse tied to the tree, I found
the road, went about a hundred yards around the point of a hill,
and saw the camp-fire up in a little flat about a quarter of a mile
from where I had spent the night. Going up to camp, I found the
men all standing around a fire they had made, where two large pines
had fallen across each other. They had laid down pine bark and
pieces of wood to keep them out of the water. They had stood up
all night. The water was running two or three inches deep all through
the camp. When I got to the fire, and began to get warm, my legs
and arms began to swell so that I could hardly move or get my
hands to my face.

"It never ceased raining all that day nor the next night, and we
were obliged to stand around the fire. Everything we had was wet.
They had stacked up our dried beef and flour in a pile, and put the
saddles and pack saddles over it as well as they could, but still it
got more or less wet. The third morning it stopped raining about
daylight, and the sun came out clear and warm. We made scaffolds
and spread our meat all out, hung up our blankets and clothing on

lines, and by keeping up fires and with the help of the sun, we managed to get everything dry by night. The next morning we packed up and started on until we came to a little valley, when we found some grass for our horses. We stayed there that night. The next day we got to Steep Hollow Creek, one of the branches of Bear River. This stream was not more than a hundred feet wide, but it was about twenty feet deep, and the current was very swift. We felled a large pine tree across it, but the center swayed down so that the water ran over it about a foot deep. We tied ropes together and stretched them across to make a kind of hand railing, and succeeded in carrying over all our things. We undertook to make our horses swim the creek, and finally forced two of them into the stream, but as soon as they struck the current they were carried down faster than we could run. One of them at last reached the bank and got ashore, but the other went down under the tree we had cut, and the first we saw of him he came up about twenty yards below heels upward. He finally struck a drift about a hundred yards below, and we succeeded in getting him out almost drowned. We then tied ropes together, part of the men went over, and tying a rope to each horse, those on one side would force him into the water, and the others would draw him across. We lost a half day at this place. That night we climbed a high mountain, and came to snow. Camped that night without any feed for our horses. The next day, about noon, we reached Mule Springs. The snow was from three to four feet deep, and it was impossible to go any farther with the horses. Unpacking the animals, Joe Varro and Wm. Eddy started back with them to Johnson's ranch. The rest of us went to work and built a brush tent in which to keep our provisions. We set forks into the ground, laid poles across, and covered them with cedar boughs. We finished them that evening, and the next morning ten of the men fixed up their packs, consisting of dried beef and flour, and started on foot, each one carrying about seventy-five pounds. They left Billy Coon and myself to watch the provisions until they returned. I have never been in that country since, but I think Mule Springs is on the opposite side of Bear River from Dutch Flat.

"After the men had all gone I amused myself the first day by getting wood and cutting cedar limbs to finish our camp with. My companion, Billy Coon, was partially insane, and was no company at all. He would get up in the morning, eat his food and then lie down and sleep for two or three hours. He would only talk when he was spoken to; and all he knew was to sleep and eat. I got very lonesome, and would sit for hours thinking of our situation. Sixty miles from any human habitation! Surrounded with wild Indians and wild beasts! Then, when I would look away at the snow-capped peaks of the Sierras, and think that my father and the rest of the men were there, toiling under the heavy loads which they carried, I became still more gloomy. When night would come, the big gray wolves that had collected on the mountains facing to the south, where the snow had melted off, would set up their howlings. This, with the dismal sound of the wind roaring through the tall pine trees, was almost unendurable. To this day, when I am in pine timber, and hear the wind sighing through the tree-tops, I always think of the Donner Party and of those lonely days in the mountains.

"The third day after the men left I became so lonesome that I took the gun and went down in the direction in which I had heard the wolves howling. When I got down out of the snow I found the deer had collected there by the hundreds. I killed two deer; went up and got Billy Coon, and we carried them up to camp. We hung one on each corner of our brush tent, not more than six feet from our bed and not more than four feet from the fire. Next morning one of the deer was gone! I suppose the Indians had found us out and stolen it; but when I looked for tracks I found the thief had been a California lion. I tracked him two or three hundred yards, but he had walked off with the deer so easily I thought he might keep it. That afternoon I went down to kill another deer, but when I reached a point from which I could see down to the river, I saw the smoke of an Indian camp. I was afraid to shoot for fear the

Indians would hear the gun, and finding out we were there, would come up and give us trouble. I started back, and when in sight of camp I sat down on a log to rest. While sitting there I saw three Indians coming up the hill. I sat still to see what they would do. They came up to within sight of camp and all crawled up behind a large sugar-pine tree and sat there watching the camp. I did not like their movements, so thought I would give them a scare. I leveled the old gun at the tree, about six feet above their heads, and fired away. They got away from there faster than they came, and I never saw them afterwards.

"On the fifth day after the men left, three of them came back to the camp. They informed me they had been three days in traveling from Mule Springs to Bear Valley, a distance of twelve miles. These three had found it impossible to stand the journey, but the other seven had started on from Bear Valley. It was thought they could never get over to Truckee Lake, for the snow was so soft it was impossible to carry their heavy loads through from ten to thirty feet of it."

M. D. Ritchie and R. P. Tucker kept a diary of the journey of the first relief party, which, thanks to Patty Reed, now Mrs. Frank Lewis, is before us. It is brief, concise, pointed, and completes the narration of Mr. George W. Tucker. Mr. Ritchie's diary reads :

"Feb. 5, 1847. First day traveled ten miles. Bad roads; often miring down horses and mules. On the 6th and 7th traveled fifteen miles. Road continued bad ; commenced raining before we got to camp, and continued to rain all that day and night very severe. Laid by here on the 8th to dry our provisions and clothing.

"Feb. 9. Traveled fifteen miles. Swam the animals over one creek, and carried the provisions over on a log.

"Feb. 10. Traveled four miles ; came to the snow ; continued about four miles further. Animals floundering in snow, and camped at the Mule Springs.

"Feb. 11. Mr. Eddy started back with the animals; left William Coon and George Tucker to guard what provisions were left in camp; the other ten men, each taking about fifty pounds, except

Mr. Curtis, who took about twenty-five pounds.   Traveled on through the snow, having a very severe day's travel over mountains, making about six miles.   Camped on Bear River, near a cluster of large pines.

"Feb. 12.   Moved camp about two miles, and stopped to make snow-shoes; tried them on and found them of no benefit; cast them away.

"Feb. 13.   Made Bear Valley.   Upon digging for Curtis' wagon found the snow ten feet deep, and the provisions destroyed by the bears.   Rain and snow fell on us all night."

By Curtis' wagon is meant a cache made by Reed and McCutchen, which will be described in the next chapter.

"Feb. 14.   Fine weather."

From this time forward the journal was kept by Captain Reasin P. Tucker.

"Feb. 15.   Fine day.   Three of our men decline going any further—W. D. Ritchie, A. Brueheim and James Curtis.   Only seven men being left, the party was somewhat discouraged.   We consulted together, and under existing circumstances I took it upon myself to insure every man who persevered to the end, five dollars per day from the time they entered the snow.   We determined to go ahead, and camped to-night on Yuba River, after traveling fifteen miles.

"Feb. 16.   Traveling very bad and snowing.   Made but five miles, and camped in snow fifteen feet deep.

"Feb. 17.   Traveled five miles.

"Feb. 18.   Traveled eight miles, and camped on the head of the Yuba; on the pass we suppose the snow to be thirty feet deep."

The "pass" was the Summit.   Relief was close at hand.   Would it find the emigrants?

CHAPTER XI.

AMES F. REED encountered the most disheartening trials after leaving the Donner Party. He and Walter Herron were reduced to the utmost verge of starvation while on the Sierra Nevadas. At one time they discovered five beans in the road, one after the other; and at another time, they ate of the rancid tallow which was found in a tar bucket under an old wagon.

Mr. Reed has told the rest in an article contributed by him to the Rural Press. It explains, so well, the difficulties of getting relief to the emigrants, that it is copied:

"When I arrived at Captain Sutter's, making known my situation to him, asking if he would furnish me horses and saddles to bring the women and children out of the mountains (I expected to meet them at the head of Bear Valley by the time I could return there), he at once complied with the request, also saying that he would do everything possible for me and the company. On the evening of my arrival at the Captain's, I found Messrs. Bryant, Lippencott, Grayson and Jacobs, some of the early voyagers in the

Russel Company, they having left that company at Fort Laramie, most of them coming on horseback.

"During the evening a meeting was held, in which I participated, adopting a memorial to the commander of Sutter's Fort, to raise one or more companies of volunteers, to proceed to Los Angeles, we being at war with Mexico at this time. The companies were to be officered by the petitioners. Being requested to take command of one of the companies, I declined, stating that it would be necessary for the Captain to stay with the company; also that I had to return to the mountains for the emigrants, but that I would take a Lieutenantcy. This was agreed to, and I was on my return to the emigrants to enlist all the men I could between there and Bear Valley. On my way up I enlisted twelve or thirteen.

"The second night after my arrival at Captain Sutter's we had a light rain; next morning we could see snow on the mountains. The Captain stated that it was low down and heavy for the first fall of the season. The next day I started on my return with what horses and saddles Captain Sutter had to spare. He furnished us all the flour needed, and a hind quarter of beef, giving us an order for more horses and saddles at Mr. Cordway's, near where Marysville is located. In the meantime Mr. McCutchen joined us, he being prevented from returning with Mr. Stanton on account of sickness. After leaving Mr. Johnson's ranch we had thirty horses, one mule, and two Indians to help drive.

"Nothing happened until the evening before reaching the head of Bear Valley, when there commenced a heavy rain and sleet, continuing all night. We drove on until a late hour before halting. We secured the flour and horses, the rain preventing us from kindling a fire. Next morning, proceeding up the valley to where we were to take the mountain, we found a tent containing a Mr. Curtis and wife. They hailed us as angels sent for their delivery, stating that they would have perished had it not been for our arrival. Mrs. Curtis stated that they had killed their dog, and at the time of our arrival had the last piece in the Dutch oven baking. We told them not to be alarmed about anything to eat, for we had plenty, both of flour and beef, and that they were welcome to all they needed. Our appetites were rather keen, not having eaten anything from the morning previous. Mr. Curtis remarked that in the oven was a piece of the dog and we could have it. Raising the lid of the oven we found the dog well baked, and having a fine savory smell. I cut out a rib, smelling and tasting, found it to be good, handed it over to McCutchen, who, after smelling it some time, tasted it and pronounced it very good dog. We partook of Curtis' dog. Mrs. Curtis immediately commenced making bread, and in a short time had supper for all.

"At the lower end of the valley where we entered the snow was eighteen inches in depth, and when we arrived at the tent it was two feet. Curtis stated that his oxen had taken the back track, and that he had followed them by the trail through the snow. In the morning before leaving, Mrs. Curtis got us to promise to take them into the settlement when on our return with the women and children. Before leaving, we gave them flour and beef sufficient to keep them until our return, expecting to do so in a few days.

"We started, following the trail made by the oxen, and camped a number of miles up the mountain. In the night, hearing some of the horses going down the trail, we went to the spot where the Indians had lain down, and found them gone. McCutchen mounted his horse and rode down to Curtis' camp, and found that the Indians had been there, stopped and warmed themselves, and then started down the valley. He returned to camp about the middle of the night.

"Next morning we started, still on the trail of the oxen, but unfortunately, the trail turned off to the left from our direction. We proceeded on, the snow deepening rapidly, our horses struggling to get through; we pushed them on until they would rear upon their hind feet to breast the snow, and when they would alight they would sink in it until nothing was seen of them but the nose and a portion of the head. Here we found that it was utterly impossible to proceed further with the horses. Leaving them, we proceeded further on foot, thinking that we could get in to the people, but found that impossible, the snow being soft and deep.

"I may here state that neither of us knew anything about snow-shoes, having always lived in a country where they never were used.

"With sorrowful hearts, we arrived that night at the camp of Mr. Curtis, telling them to make their arrangements for leaving with us in the morning. Securing our flour in the wagon of Mr. Curtis, so that we could get it on our return, we packed one horse with articles belonging to Mr. and Mrs. Curtis, and started down the valley to where the snow was light, and where there was considerable underbrush, so that our famished animals could browse, they not having eaten anything for several days.

"After packing Mr. Curtis' horse for him the next morning, we started; in a short time, Mr. and Mrs. Curtis proceeded ahead, leaving the pack-horse behind for us to drive, instead of his leading him; we having our hands full in driving the loose ones, they scattering in all directions. The pack turned on the horse. Mr. Curtis was requested to return and help repack and lead his horse, but he paid no attention to us. We stood this for some time; finally McCutchen became angry, started after him, determined to bring him back; when he got with him he paid no attention to McCutchen's request to return; Mac becoming more exasperated, hit him several times over the shoulders with his riatta. This brought him to his senses. He said that if Mac would not kill him he would come back and take care of the pack animal, and he did.

"As soon as we arrived at Captain Sutter's, I made a statement of all the circumstances attending our attempt to get into the mountains. He was no way surprised at our defeat. I also gave the Captain the number of head of cattle the company had when I left them. He made an estimate and stated that if the emigrants would kill the cattle and place the meat in the snow for preservation, there was no fear of starvation until relief could reach them. He further stated that there were no able-bodied men in that vicinity, all having gone down the country with and after Fremont to fight the Mexicans.

He advised me to proceed to Yerba Buena, now San Francisco, and make my case known to the naval officer in command.

" I left Captain Sutter's by the way of San Jose, for San Francisco, being unable to come by water. When I arrived at San Jose I found the San Francisco side of the bay was occupied by the Mexicans. Here I remained, and was attached to a company of volunteers, commanded by Captain Webber, until after the fight at Santa Clara.

" The road now being clear I proceeded to San Francisco with a petition from some of the prominent citizens of San Jose, asking the commander of the navy to grant aid to enable me to return to the mountains."

It is proper, perhaps, to interrupt the narrative in the Rural Press for the purpose of introducing the memorial referred to by Mr. Reed. The copy of the original document was recently found among his papers by his daughter, Patty Reed:

"To his Excellency, R. F. Stockton, Governor and Commander-in-Chief by sea and land of the United States Territory of California: We, the undersigned citizens and residents of the Territory of California, beg leave respectfully to present to your Excellency the following memorial, viz.: That, whereas, the last detachment of emigrants from the United States to California have been unable, from unavoidable causes, to reach the frontier settlements, and are now in the California mountains, seventy-five or one hundred miles east from the Sacramento Valley, surrounded by snow, most probably twenty feet deep, and being about eighty souls in number, a large proportion of whom are women and children, who must shortly be in a famishing condition from scarcity of provisions; therefore, the undersigned most earnestly beseech your Excellency to take into consideration the propriety of fitting out an expedition to proceed on snow-shoes immediately to the relief of the sufferers. Your memorialists beg leave to subscribe themselves, very respectfully, yours, etc.

" January, 1847."

The article in the Rural Press continues : "Arriving at San Francisco, I presented my petition to Commodore Hull, also making a statement of the condition of the people in the mountains as far as I knew, the number of them, and what would be needed in provisions and help to get them out. He made an estimate of the expense, and said that he would do anything within reason to further the object, but was afraid that the department at Washington would not sustain him if he made the general outfit. His sympathy was that of a man and a gentleman.

"I also conferred with several of the citizens of Yerba Buena; their advice was not to trouble the Commodore further; that they would call a meeting of the citizens and see what could be done. At the meeting the situation of the people was made known, and committees were appointed to collect money. Over a thousand dollars was raised in the town, and the sailors of the fleet gave over three hundred dollars. At the meeting Midshipman Woodworth volunteered to go into the mountains. Commodore Hull gave me authority to raise as many men, with horses, as would be required. The citizens purchased all the supplies necessary for the outfit, and placed them on board the schooner ———, for Hardy's Ranch, mouth of Feather River. Midshipman Woodworth took charge of the schooner, and was the financial agent of the government.

"I left in a boat for Napa by way of Sonoma, to procure men and horses, and when I arrived at Mr. Gordon's, on Cache Creek, I had all the men and horses needed. From here I proceeded to the mouth of Feather River for the purpose of meeting Mr. Woodworth with the provisions. When we reached the river the boat had not arrived. The water was very high in the river, the tule lands being overflowed. From here I sent a man to a point on the Sacramento River opposite Sutter's Fort, to obtain information of the boat with our provisions; he returned and reported the arrival of the boat at the Fort.

"Before leaving Yerba Buena, news came of a party of fifteen per-

7

sons having started from the emigrant encampment and only seven getting in to Johnson's.   I was here placed in a quandary—no boat to take us across the river, and no provisions for our party to take into the mountains.   We camped a short distance back from the river, where we killed a number of elk, for the purpose of using the skins in covering a skeleton boat.   Early next morning we started for the river, and to our delight saw a small schooner, belonging to Perry McCan, which had arrived during the night.   We immediately crossed, McCutchen and myself, tb the opposite bank of the river. I directed the men to cross and follow us to Johnson's ranch.   We arrived there early that day.   Making known our situation, he drove his cattle up to the house, saying, 'there are the cattle, take as many as you need.'   We shot down five head, staid up all night, and with the help of Mr. Johnson and his Indians, by the time the men arrived the next morning, we had the meat fire-dried and ready to be placed in bags.   Mr. Johnson had a party of Indians making flour by hand mills, they making during the night nearly two hundred pounds.

"We packed up immediately and started.   After reaching the snow, the meat and flour was divided into suitable packs for us to carry, we leaving the horses here.   At Johnson's I learned that a relief party had passed in a few days previous, being sent by Captain Sutter and Mr. Sinclair."

This was the party commanded by Captain Reasin P. Tucker, whose journey over the mountains as far as the summit was described in the last chapter.   Reed was faithful and energetic in endeavoring to recross the mountains.   Mr. McCutchen, also, did all in his power to reach the wife and baby he left behind.   The snow belt is about four times as wide on the west side of the summit as it is on the east side.   It was almost impossible for relief parties to cross the mountains.   Captain Tucker's party were composed of men of great nerve and hardihood, yet, as will be seen, the trip was almost as much as their lives were worth.

On the morning of the 19th of February, 1847, the relief party of Captain R. P. Tucker began the descent of the gorge leading to Donner Lake.

Let us glance ahead at the picture soon to be unfolded to their gaze. The mid-winter snows had almost concealed the cabins. The inmates lived subterranean lives. Steps cut in the icy snow led up from the doorways to the surface. Deep despair had settled upon all hearts. The dead were lying all around, some even unburied, and nearly all with only a covering of snow. So weak and powerless had the emigrants become, that it was hardly possible for them to lift the dead bodies up the steps out of the cabins. All were reduced to mere skeletons. They had lived on pieces of raw-hide, or on old cast-away bones which were boiled or burned until they could be eaten, and they were so reduced that it seemed as if only a dry, shriveled skin covered their emaciated frames. The eyes were sunken deep in their sockets, and had a fierce, ghastly, demoniacal look. The faces were haggard, woe-begone, and sepulchral. One seldom heard the sound of a voice, and when heard, it was weak, tremulous, pitiful. Sometimes a child would moan and sob for a mouthful of food, and the poor, helpless mothers, with breaking hearts, would have to soothe them, as best they could, with kind words and tender caresses. Food, there was none. Oh! what words can fitly frame a tribute for those noble mothers! When strong men gave up, and passively awaited the delirium of death, the mothers were actively administering to the wants of the dying, and striving to cheer and comfort the living. Marble monuments never bore more heroic names than those of Margaret W. Reed, Lavina Murphy, Elizabeth Graves, Margaret Breen, Tamsen Donner, and Elizabeth Donner. Their charity, fortitude, and self-sacrifice failed not in the darkest hour. Death came so often now, that little notice was taken of his approach save by these mothers. A dreadful want of consciousness precedes starvation. The actual death is not so terrible. The delirious would rave of feasts, and rich viands, and bountiful stores of food. As the shadows of death more closely enveloped the poor creatures, the mutterings grew unintelligible, and were interrupted now and then by startled cries of phrensy, which gradually grew fainter until the victims finally slumbered. From this slumber there was no awakening. The breathing became feebler and more irregular, and finally ceased.   It was not so terrible to the unconscious dying, as to weeping mother who watched by the sufferer's side.

It was always dark and gloomy enough in the snow-covered cabins, but during the fierce, wild storms, the desolation became almost unendurable.   The rushing gale, the furious storm, the lashing of storm-rent pine boughs, or the crash of giant trees overthrown by the hurricane, filled the souls of the imprisoned emigrants with name-less dread.   Sometimes the silent darkness of the night would shudder with the howl of the great gray wolves which in those days infested the mountains.   Too well did they know that these gaunt beasts were howling for the bodies of the living as well as of the dead.

Wood grew plentifully at short distances from the cabins, but for these weak, starving creatures to obtain it was a herculean task.   To go out when the storms were raging would be almost impossible for a well, strong man.   To struggle through the deep, loose drifts, reaching frequently to the waist, required at any time fearful exertion. The numb, fleshless fingers could hardly guide, or even wield the ax. Near the site of the Breen cabin, to-day, stands a silent witness of the almost superhuman exertions that were made to procure fuel. On the side of a pine tree are old seams and gashes, which by their irregular position, were evidently made by hands too weak to cut down a tree.   Hundreds of blows, however, had been struck, and the marks of the ax-blade extend up and down the side of the tree for a foot and a half.   Bark seared with age has partly covered por-tions of the cuts, but in one place the incision is some inches deep. At the foot of this pine was found a short, decayed ax-handle, and a broad bladed, old-fashioned ax-head.   The mute story of these wit-nesses is unmistakable.   The poor starved being who undertook the task, never succeeded.

Trees felled, frequently buried themselves out of sight in the loose snow, or at best, only the uppermost branches could be obtained. Without fire, without food, without proper shelter from the dampness occasioned by the melting snows, in the bitter, biting wintry weather, the men, women, and children were huddled together, the living and the dead. When Milton Elliott died, there were no men to assist in removing the body from the deep pit. Mrs. Reed and her daughter Virginia bravely undertook the task. Tugging, pushing, lifting as best they could, the corpse was raised up the icy steps. He died in the Murphy cabin by the rock. A few days before he died, he crawled over to the Breen cabin, where were Mrs. Reed and her children. For years he had been one of the members of this family. He worked for Mr. Reed in the mill and furniture establishment owned by the latter in Jamestown, Illinois. He drove the same yoke of oxen, " Bully " and " George," who were the wheel-oxen of Reed's family team on the plains. When Mr. Reed proposed crossing the plains, his wife and children refused to go unless Milt. could be induced to drive. He was a kind, careful man, and after Mr. Reed had been driven away from the company, Elliott always provided for them as best he was able. Now that he was going to die, he wanted to see " Ma " and the children once more. " Ma " was the term he always used in addressing Mrs. Reed. None realized better than he the sorrowful position in which she was placed by having no husband upon whom to lean in this time of great need. Poor Elliott, he knew that he was starving! starving! " Ma, I am not going to starve to death, I am going to eat of the bodies of the dead." This was what he told Mrs. Reed, yet when he attempted to do so, his heart revolted at the thought. Mrs. Reed accompanied him a portion of the way back to the Murphy cabin, and before leaving him knelt on the snow and prayed as only a mother can, that the Good Father would help them in this hour of distress. It was a starving Christian mother praying that relief might come to her starving children, and especially to this, her starving boy. From the granite rocks, the solemn forests, and the snow-mantled mountains of Donner Lake, a more fervent prayer never ascended heavenward. Could Elliott have heard, in his dying moments, that this prayer was soon to be answered so far as Mrs. Reed and her little ones were concerned, he would have welcomed death joyfully.

As time wore wearily on, another and more severe trial awaited

Mrs. Reed. Her daughter Virginia was dying. The innutritious raw-hide was not sufficient to sustain life in the poor famished body of the delicate child. Indeed, toward the last, her system became so debilitated that she found it impossible to eat the loathsome, glue-like preparation which formed their only food. Silently she had endured her sufferings, until she was at the very portals of death. This beautiful girl was a great favorite of Mrs. Breen's. Oftentimes during the days of horror and despair, this good Irish mother had managed, unobserved, to slip an extra piece of meat or morsel of food to Virginia. Mrs. Breen was the first to discover that the mark of death was visible upon the girl's brow. In order to break the news to Mrs. Reed, without giving those in the cabin a shock which might prove fatal, Mrs. Breen asked the mother up out of the cabin on the crisp white snow.

It was the evening of the 19th of February, 1847. The sun was setting, and his rays, in long lance-like lines sifted through the darkening forests. Far to the eastward, the summits of the Washoe mountains lay bathed in golden sun-light, while the deep gorges at their feet were purpling into night. The gentle breeze which crept over the bosom of the ice-bound lake softly wafted from the tree-tops a muffled dirge for the dying girl. Ere another day dawned over the expanse of snow, her spirit would pass to a haven of peace, where the demons of famine could never enter.

In the desolate cabin, all was silence. Living under the snow, passing an underground life as it were, seldom visiting each other, or leaving the cabins, these poor prisoners learned to listen, rather than look for relief. During the first days they watched hour after hour the upper end of the lake where the "fifteen" had disappeared. With aching eyes and weary hearts, they always turned back to their subterranean abodes disappointed. Hope finally deserted the strongest hearts. The brave mothers had constantly encouraged the despondent by speaking of the promised relief, yet this was prompted more by the necessities of the situation than from any belief that help would arrive. It was human nature, however, to glance toward the towering summits whenever they ascended to the surface of the snow, and to listen at all times for an unfamiliar sound or footstep. So delicate became their sense of hearing, that every noise of the wind, every visitor's tread, every sound that ordinarily occurred above their heads, was known and instantly detected.

On this evening, as the two women were sobbing despairingly upon the snow, the silence of the twilight was broken by a shout from near Donner Lake ! In an instant every person forgot weakness and infirmity, and clambered up the stairway ! It was a strange voice, and in the distance they discovered strange forms approaching. The Reed and the Breen children thought, at first, that it was a band of Indians, but Patrick Breen, the good old father, soon declared that the strangers were white men. Captain Tucker and his men had found the wide expanse of snow covering forest and valley, and had shouted to attract attention, if any of the emigrants yet survived. Oh! what joy ! There were tears in other eyes than those of the little children. The strongest men in the relief party sat down on the snow and wept with the rest. It is related of one or two mothers, and can readily be believed, that their first act was to fall upon their knees, and with faces turned to God, to pour out their gratitude to Him for having brought assistance to their dying children. Virginia Reed did not die.

Captain Reasin P. Tucker, who had been acquainted with the Graves family on the plains before the Donner Party took the Hastings Cut-off, was anxious to meet them. They lived in the lower cabin, half a mile further down Donner Creek. When he came close enough to observe the smoke issuing from the hole in the snow which marked their abode, he shouted, as he had done at the upper cabins. The effect was as electrical as in the former instance. All came up to the surface, and the same unrestrained gladness was manifested by the famished prisoners. Famished they were. Mrs. Graves is especially praised by the survivors for her unstinted charity. Instead of selfishly hoarding her stores and feeding only her own children, she was generous to a fault, and no person ever asked at her door for food who did not receive as good as she and her little ones had to eat.

Dear Mrs. Graves! How earnestly she asked about her husband and daughters. Did all reach the valley? Captain Tucker felt his heart rise in his throat. How could he tell this weak, starved woman of the terrible fate which had befallen her husband and her son-in-law! He could not! He answered with assumed cheerfulness in the affirmative. So, too, they deceived Mrs. Murphy regarding her dear boy Lemuel. It was best. Had the dreadful truth been told, not one of all this company would ever had courage to attempt the dangerous journey.

Little sleep was there in the Donner cabins that night. The relief party were to start back in a couple of days, and such as were strong enough were to accompany them. Mrs. Graves had four little children, and told her son William C. Graves that he must remain with her to cut wood to keep the little ones from freezing. But William was anxious to go and help send back provisions to his mother. So earnestly did he work during the next two days, that he had two cords of wood piled up near the cabin. This was to last until he could return. His task was less difficult because the cabin was built in a dense grove of tamarack.

Food had been given in small quantities to the sufferers. Many of the snow-bound prisoners were so near death's door that a hearty meal would have proven fatal. The remnant of provisions brought by the relief party was carefully guarded lest some of the famished wretches should obtain more than was allotted them. This was rendered easier from the fact that the members of the relief party were unable to endure the scenes of misery and destitution in the cabins, and so camped outside upon the snow. So hungry were the poor people that some of them ate the strings of the snow-shoes which part of the relief company had brought along.

On the 20th of February, John Rhodes, R. S. Mootry and R. P. Tucker visited the Donner tents on Alder Creek, seven miles from the cabins. Only one ox hide remained to these destitute beings. Here, as well as at the cabins, the all-important question was, who should go with the relief party and who remain. In each family there were little children who could not go unless carried. Few of

the Donner Party had more than strength enough to travel unen-
cumbered across the deep snows. Should a storm occur on the
mountains, it was doubtful if even the members of the relief party
could escape death. It was hopefully urged that other relief parties
would soon arrive from California, and that these would bring over
those who remained. In determining who should go and who stay,
examples of heroism and devotion were furnished which were never
surpassed in the history of man. Could their vision have penetrated
the veil which interposed between them and the sad occurrences
about to ensue, they would have known that almost every family,
whose members separated, was bidding good-bye to some member
forever.

Chapter XII.

RS. TAMSEN DONNER was well and comparatively
strong, and could easily have crossed the mountains in
safety with this party. Her husband, however, was suffering from a serious swelling on one of his hands. Sometime before reaching the mountains he had accidentally
hurt this hand while handling a wagon. After encamping
at Alder Creek he was anxious to assist in the arrangements and
preparations for Winter, and in using his hand the old wound
reopened. Taking cold in the hand, it became greatly swollen and
inflamed, and he was rendered entirely helpless. Mrs. Donner was
urged to go with the relief party, but resolutely determined to heed
the promptings of wifely devotion and remain by her husband.

No one will ever read the history of the Donner Party without
greatly loving and reverencing the character of this faithful wife.
The saddest, most tear-stained page of the tragedy, relates to her life
and death in the mountains. A better acquaintance with the Donner
family, and especially with Mrs. Tamsen Donner, cannot fail to be
desirable in view of succeeding chapters. Thanks to Mr. Allen
Francis, the present American Consul at Victoria, British Columbia,

very complete, authentic and interesting information upon this subject has been furnished. Mr. Francis was publisher of the Springfield (Illinois,) Journal in 1846, and a warm personal friend of the family.

The Donners were among the first settlers of Sangamon County, Illinois. They were North Carolinians, immigrants to Kentucky in 1818, subsequently to the State of Indiana, and from thence to what was known as the Sangamon Country in the year 1828.

George Donner was about six feet in height, large, and a fine looking man, of good sense and much general information ; one to whom his friends and neighbors came to ask respecting their farms and herds, and they usually went home feeling that they had been properly advised. He possessed a cheerful disposition and easy temperament, merry black eyes, and blackest of hair, which was lined with an occasional silver thread. He was an honest, generous, good-natured man, whom nearly every one liked, and no one cared to find faults in " Uncle George." He was married three times, and was the father of a large family. Tamsen, his third wife, was about five feet in height, her weight was ninety-six pounds, her eyes were grayish blue, hair brown, her face was not pretty, but was full of character and intelligence, her movements were energetic, but her manner was composed, dignified and ladylike. Her dress was of the best of material, but noted for its Quaker simplicity. Her conversation was fascinating, and her voice would hold its listeners in perfect silence for hours while she read. Even those who did not fail to criticise her ignorance of farm and dairy work, were often charmed and softened by her voice and absence of display. Her maiden name was Tamsen Eustis, and she was born in Newburyport, Mass., in 1801. Her love of books made her a student at an early age; almost as soon as the baby dimples left her cheeks, she sought the school-room, which afforded her great enjoyment. Her mother's death, which occurred before she was seven years old, was her first real grief, and for a time she seemed overwhelmed with sadness; but the sympathy of friends and her thirst for knowledge soothed and led her back to the school-room, where she pursued her studies with more eagerness than before.

Her father married again, and little Tamsen's life was rendered happier by this event, for in her step-mother she found a friend who kindly advised her movements and encouraged her work. At fifteen years of age she had finished the course of study, and her proficiency in higher mathematics, geometry, philosophy, etc., called forth the greatest praise of her teachers and learned friends. She, like many daughters of New England, realized that talent was given to be used, and that every life was created for some definite purpose. She resolved to devote herself to the instruction of the young. She taught for a time in Newburyport, then received a call to fill a vacancy in the academy in Elizabeth City, N. C., which she accepted, and where she continued an earnest and appreciated teacher for a number of years. She became a fluent French scholar at this institution, and devoted her leisure hours to the fine arts. Her paintings and drawings were much admired for their correctness of outline and subdued colors and delicacy in shading.

In Elizabeth City she met Mr. Dozier, a young man of education and good family. They were married. Mr. Dozier was not a man of means, but her forethought enabled them to live comfortably. For a few brief years she enjoyed all the happiness which wedded bliss and maternal love could give. Then came death, and in a few short weeks her husband and two children were snatched from her arms. In her desolation and grief she thought of her old home, and longed for the sympathy of her childhood's friends. She returned to Newburyport and spent three years in retirement and rest. Then, in 1836, came an urgent request from her brother in Illinois, for her to come to his afflicted household, and teach his motherless children. She remained with them one Winter, but her field of action had been too wide to permit her to settle quietly on a farm, twenty-one miles from Springfield, and besides she had heard much of the manner in which country schools were conducted, and was anxious to test her ability in controlling and teaching a country school. She obtained a school in Auburn, and soon became the friend of her pupils. All agreed that Mrs. Dozier was a faithful teacher, until the following little incident occurred.

The worthy Board of School Trustees had heard that Mrs. Dozier was in the habit of knitting during school hours. "Surely she could not knit, and instruct her pupils properly, therefore she must either give up her school or her knitting." When Mrs. Dozier heard their resolution she smiled and said: "Before those gentlemen deny my ability to impart knowledge and work with my fingers at the same time, I would like them to visit my school, and judge me by the result of their observation."

A knock at the school-room door a week later, startled the children, a committee of trustees entered, and Mrs. Dozier received and seated them in the most ladylike manner. Then she called class after class, recitations were heard and explained while the knitting went steadily on. For hours those gentlemen sat in silence; the teacher was too busy to be interrupted, and they were interested in all that transpired. When the hour for closing school arrived, she invited the gentlemen to address her pupils, after which she dismissed her school, thanked her visitors for their kind attention, and went home without getting their opinion.

The next morning she was informed that the Board of Trustees had met the previous evening to hear the report of the visiting committee, and after hearing the report, the Board had unanimously agreed that "Mrs. Dozier shall keep her school and her knitting too." This little triumph was much enjoyed by her friends.

The next year she was urged to take the school at Sugar Creek, where the pupils were further advanced and much older than those at Auburn. Her connection with this school marked a new era for many of its pupils. Mr. J. Miller used to relate an incident which occurred a few days after she took charge of those unruly boys, who frequently managed teacher and school to suit themselves. He said: "I never will forget how Mrs. Dozier took her seat at the table, tapped for order, and in a kind, polite, but firm voice, said: 'Young gentlemen and young ladies, as a teacher only, I cannot criticise the propriety of your writing notes to each other when out of school; but as your teacher, with full authority in school, I desire and request you neither to write nor send notes to any one during

school hours.   I was surprised and grieved at your conduct yesterday, and should my wish be disregarded in the future I will be
obliged to chastise the offender.'   She then tapped for the first class,
and school began in earnest.   I looked at her quiet face and diminu-
tive form, and thought how easy it would be for me to pick up two or
three such little bodies as she and set them outside the door !   I
wrote a note and threw it to the pupil in front of me, just to try Mrs.
Dozier.   When the recitation was finished, she stepped to the side
of her table, and looking at me with such a grieved expression on
her face, said : 'Mr. Miller, I regret that my oldest scholar should
be the first to violate my rule.   Please step forward.'   I quailed beneath her eye.   I marched up to where she stood.   The stillness of
that school-room was oppressive.   I held out my hand at the demand
of that little woman and took the punishment I deserved, and returned to my seat deeply humiliated but fully determined to behave
myself in the future, and make the other boys do likewise.   Well, she
had no more trouble while she was our teacher.   Her pluck had won
our admiration and her quiet dignity held our respect, and we boys
ceased to wonder at the ease with which she overturned our plans
and made us eager to adopt hers; for no teacher ever taught on
Sugar Creek who won the affections and ruled pupils more easily and
happily than she.   She expected us to come right up to the mark ;
but if we got into trouble she was always ready to help us out, and
she could do it in the quietest way imaginable.   Frequently she
would wander through field and meadow with her class in surveying
and her class in botany.   She sought by creek and over plain for
specimens with which to illustrate their lessons.   It was while engaged as teacher at this place that Mrs Dozier made the acquaintance and married George Donner and moved to his home on Sugar
Creek, two miles and a half from Springfield."

Mr. Francis says : " Mrs. George Donner was a perfect type of an
eastern lady, kind, sociable and exemplary, ever ready to assist neighbors, and even the stranger in distress.   Whenever she could spare
time, she wielded a ready pen on various topics.   She frequently
contributed gems in prose and poetry to the columns of the Journal,

that awakened an interest among its readers to know their author. Herself and husband were faithful members of the German Prairie Christian Church, situated a little north of their residence. Here they lived happily and highly respected by all who knew them until the Spring of 1846, when they started for California."

Having said this much of the Donners, and especially of the noble woman who refused to leave her suffering husband, let us glance at the parting scenes at Alder Creek. It had been determined that the two eldest daughters of George Donner should accompany Captain Tucker's party. George Donner, Jr., and William Hook, two of Jacob Donner's sons, Mrs. Wolfinger, and Noah James were also to join the company. This made six from the Donner tents. Mrs. Elizabeth Donner was quite able to have crossed the mountains, but preferred to remain with her two little children, Lewis and Samuel, until another and larger relief party should arrive. These two boys were not large enough to walk, Mrs. Donner was not strong enough to carry them, and the members of Captain Tucker's party had already agreed to take as many little ones as they could carry.

Leanna C. Donner, now Mrs. John App, of Jamestown, Tuolumne County, Cal., gives a vivid description of the trip from George Donner's tent to the cabins at Donner Lake. Miss Rebecca E. App, acting as her mother's amanuensis, writes:

" Mother says: ' Never shall I forget the day when my sister Elitha and myself left our tent. Elitha was strong and in good health, while I was so poor and emaciated that I could scarcely walk. All we took with us were the clothes on our backs and one thin blanket, fastened with a string around our necks, answering the purpose of a shawl in the day-time, and which was all we had to cover us at night. We started early in the morning, and many a good cry I had before we reached the cabins, a distance of about eight miles. Many a time I sat down in the snow to die, and would have perished there if my sister had not urged me on, saying, ' The cabins are just over the hill.' Passing over the hill, and not seeing the cabins, I would give up, again sit down and have another cry, but my sister continued to help and encourage me until I saw the smoke rising from the cabins;

then I took courage, and moved along as fast as I could.   When we reached the Graves cabin it was all I could do to step down the snow steps into the cabin.   Such pain and misery as I endured that day is beyond description."

In Patrick Breen's diary are found the following entries, which allude to Captain Tucker's relief party:

"Feb. 19.   Froze hard last night.   Seven men arrived from California yesterday with provisions, but left the greater part on the way. To-day it is clear and warm for this region; some of the men have gone to Donner's camp; they will start back on Monday.

"Feb. 22.   The Californians started this morning, twenty-three in number, some in a very weak state.   Mrs. Keseberg started with them, and left Keseberg here, unable to go.   Buried Pike's child this morning in the snow; died two days ago."

Poor little Catherine Pike lingered until this time!   It will be remembered that this little nursing babe had nothing to eat except a little coarse flour mixed in snow water.   Its mother crossed the mountains with the Forlorn Hope, and from the 16th of December to the 20th of February it lived upon the miserable gruel made from unbolted flour.   How it makes the heart ache to think of this little sufferer, wasting away, moaning with hunger, and sobbing for something to eat.   The teaspoonful of snow water would contain only a few particles of the flour, yet how eagerly the dying child would reach for the pitiful food.   The tiny hands grew thinner, the sad, pleading eyes sank deeper in their fleshless sockets, the face became hollow, and the wee voice became fainter, yet, day after day, little Catherine Pike continued to breathe, up to the very arrival of the relief party.

Patrick Breen says twenty-three started across the mountains. Their names were: Mrs. Margaret W. Reed and her children Virginia E. Reed, Patty Reed, Thomas Reed, and James F. Reed, Jr.; Elitha C. Donner, Leanna C. Donner, Wm. Hook, and George Donner, Jr.; Wm. G. Murphy, Mary M. Murphy, and Naomi L. Pike; Wm. C. Graves, Eleanor Graves, and Lovina Graves; Mrs. Phillipine Keseberg and Ada Keseberg; Edward J. and Simon P. Breen, Eliza Williams, John Denton, Noah James, and Mrs. Wolfinger.

In starting from the camps at Donner Lake, Mrs. Keseberg's child and Naomi L. Pike were carried by the relief party. In a beautiful letter received from Naomi L. Pike (now Mrs. Schenck, of the Dalles, Oregon), she says: "I owe my life to the kind heart of John Rhodes, whose sympathies were aroused for my mother. He felt that she was deserving of some relic of all she had left behind, when she started with the first party in search of relief, and carried me to her in a blanket." We have before spoken of this noble man's bravery in bearing the news of the condition of the " Forlorn Hope " and of the Donner Party to Sutter's Fort. Here we find him again exhibiting the nobility of his nature by saving this little girl from starvation by carrying her on his back over forty miles of wintry snow.

Before the party had proceeded two miles, a most sad occurrence took place. It became evident that Patty and Thomas Reed were unable to stand the fatigue of the journey. Already they exhibited signs of great weakness and weariness, and it was not safe to allow them to proceed. Mr. Aquilla Glover informed Mrs. Reed that it was necessary that these two children go back. Who can portray the emotions of this fond mother? What power of language can indicate the struggle which took place in the minds of this stricken family? Mr. Glover promised to return as soon as he arrived at Bear Valley, and himself bring Patty and Thomas over the mountains. This promise, however, was but a slight consolation for the agonized mother or weeping children, and finally a hopeful thought occurred to Mrs. Reed. She turned suddenly to Mr. Glover, and asked, "Are you a Mason?" He replied, " I am." " Do you promise me," she said, "upon the word of a Mason, that when you arrive at Bear Valley you will come back and get my children? " Mr. Glover made the promise, and the children were by him taken back to the cabins. The mother had remembered, in this gloomiest moment of life, that the father of her little ones was a Mason, and that he deeply reverenced the Order. If her children must be left behind in the terrible snows, she would trust the promise of this Mason to

8

return and save them.   It was a beautiful trust in a secret Order by a Mason's wife in deep distress.

Rebecca E. App, writing for her mother, Leanna C. App, nee Donner, gives a vivid description of this journey across the summits, from which is taken the following brief extract:

" It was a bright Sunday morning when we left the cabins.   Some were in good health, while others were so poor and emaciated that they could scarcely walk.   I was one of the weakest in the party, and not one in the train thought I would get to the top of the first hill.   We were a sad spectacle to look upon as we left the cabins. We marched along in single file, the leader wearing snow-shoes, and the others following after, all stepping in the leader's tracks.   I think my sister and myself were about the rear of the train, as the strongest were put in front.   My sister Elitha and I were alone with strangers, as it were, having neither father, mother, nor brothers, to give us a helping hand or a word of courage to cheer us onward.   We were placed on short allowance of food from the start, and each day this allowance was cut shorter and shorter, until we received each for our evening and morning meal two small pieces of jerked beef, about the size of the index finger of the hand.   Finally, the last ration was issued in the evening.   This was intended for that evening and the next morning, but I was so famished I could not resist the temptation to eat all I had—the two meals at one time.   Next morning, of course, I had nothing for breakfast.   Now occurred an incident which I shall never forget.   While I sat looking at the others eating their morsels of meat, which were more precious than gold or diamonds, my sister saw my distress, and divided her piece with me. How long we went without food after that, I do not know.   I think we were near the first station."

CHAPTER XIII.

HE first relief party had twenty-one emigrants with them after Patty and Thomas Reed returned to the desolate cabins. On the evening of the first day, one of the twenty-one died. It was the baby child of Lewis Keseberg. The mother had fairly worshiped her little girl. They buried the little one in the snow. It was all they could do for the pallid form of the starved little girl. Mrs. Keseberg was heart-broken over her baby's death. At the very outset she had offered everything she possessed, twenty-five dollars and a gold watch, to any one who would carry her child over the mountain. After the starved band resumed their weary march next morning, it is doubtful if many thought of the niche hollowed out of the white snow, or of the pulseless heart laid therein. Death had become fearfully common, and his victims were little heeded by the perishing company. The young German mother, however, was inconsolable. Her only boy had starved to death at the cabins, and now she was childless.

The next day the company reached Summit Valley. An incident of this day's travel illustrates the exhausted condition of the members of the Donner Party. John Denton, an Englishman, was missed when camp was pitched, and John Rhodes returned and found him fast asleep upon the snow. He had become so weary that he yielded to a slumber that would soon have proven fatal. With much labor and exertion he was aroused and brought to camp. Denton appreciated the kindness, but at the same time declared that it would be impossible for him to travel another day. Sure enough, after journeying a little way on the following morning, his strength utterly gave way. His companions built a fire for him, gave him such food as they were able, and at his earnest request continued their sorrowful march. If another relief came soon, he would, perhaps, be rescued. Denton was well educated and of good family, was a gunsmith by trade, and was skilled in metals. It is related, that while in the Graves cabin, or rather the portion of the cabin occupied by the Reeds, he discovered in the earth, ashes, and burnt stones in the fireplace, a small lump of yellowish metal, which he declared to be gold. He carefully preserved this until he left the lake, and it was doubtless lost on the mountains at his death. This was in the Spring of 1847, before the discovery of gold in California. The strange little metallic lump was exhibited to several who are yet living, and who think there is reason for believing it was really gold. A few years before the construction of the Central Pacific, Knoxville, about ten miles south of Donner Lake, and Elizabethtown, some six miles from Truckee, were famous mining camps. Gold never has been found on the very shores of Donner Lake, but should the discovery be made, and especially should gold be found in the rocks or earth near the Graves cabin, there would be reason to believe that this poor unfortunate man was in reality the first discoverer of the precious metal in California. Left alone in the snow-mantled forests of the Sierras, what were this man's emotions? In the California Star of 1847, a bound volume of which is in the State Library at Sacramento, appears the following poem. The second relief party found it written on the leaf of a memorandum book by the side of Denton's lifeless body. The pencil with which it was written lay also by the side of the unfortunate man. Ere the lethargy of death

stole away his senses, John Denton's thoughts had been of his boyhood's beautiful home in merry England.   These thoughts were
woven into verse.   Are they not strangely pathetic and beautiful?
Judge Thornton, in 1849, published them with the following prefa-
tory words : " When the circumstances are considered in connection
with the calamities in which the unhappy Denton was involved, the
whole compass of American and English poetry may be challenged
to furnish a more exquisitely beautiful, a more touching and pathetic
piece.   Simple and inornate to the last degree, yet coming from the
heart it goes to the heart.   Its lines are the last plaintive notes which
wintry winds have waked from an Æolian harp, the strings of which
rude hands have sundered.   Bring before your mind the picture of
an amiable young man who has wandered far from the paternal roof,
is stricken by famine, and left by his almost equally unhappy companions to perish among the terrible snows of the great Sierra Nevadas.   He knows that his last, most solemn hour is near.   Reason
still maintains her empire, and memory, faithful to the last, performs
her functions.   On every side extends a boundless waste of trackless
snow.   He reclines against a bank of it to rise no more, and busy
memory brings before him a thousand images of past beauty and
pleasure, and of scenes he will never revisit.   A mother's image
presents itself to his mind, tender recollections crowd upon his heart,
and the scenes of his boyhood and youth pass in review before him
with an unwonted vividness.   The hymns of praise and thanksgiving
that in harmony swelled from the domestic circle around the family
altar are remembered, and soothe the sorrows of the dying man, and
finally, just before he expires, he writes:"

> " Oh ! after many roving years,
>   How sweet it is to come
>   Back to the dwelling-place of youth,
>   Our first and dearest home ;
>   To turn away our wearied eyes
>   From proud ambition's towers,
>   And wander in those Summer fields,
>   The scenes of boyhood's hours.

" But I am changed since last I gazed
      Upon that tranquil scene,
And sat beneath the old witch elm
      That shades the village green ;
And watched my boat upon the brook—
      It was a regal galley—
And sighed not for a joy on earth,
      Beyond the happy valley.

" I wish I could once more recall
      That bright and blissful joy.
And summon to my weary heart
      The feelings of a boy.
But now on scenes of past delight
I look, and feel no pleasure,
As misers on the bed of death
      Gaze coldly on their treasure."

When Captain Tucker's relief party were going to Donner Lake, they left a portion of their provisions in Summit Valley, tied up in a tree. They had found these provisions difficult to carry, and besides, it was best to have something provided for their return, in case the famished emigrants ate all they carried over the summit. All was eaten that was taken over, and when the relief party and those they were rescuing reached the place where the provisions had been cached, all the scanty allowances had been consumed. To their horror and dismay, they found that wild animals had gnawed the ropes by which the cache had been suspended, and had destroyed every vestige of the provisions. Death stared them in the face, and the strongest men trembled at the prospect.

But aid soon arrived. James F. Reed and the little party with him met the emigrants on the 25th of February. The meeting between Reed and his family can better be imagined than described. For months they had been separated. While the father was battling with fate in endeavoring to reach California and return with assistance, the mother had been using every exertion to obtain food for her starving children. Now they met in the mountains, in the deep snows, amid pathless forests, at a time when the mother and children were out of provisions and ready to perish. Of James F. Reed be it ever remembered that he brought relief to this first relief at a time when all food was gone, and despair was fast settling down upon every heart. After greeting his wife, Virginia, and his boy James, Mr. Reed immediately passed on toward the cabins to rescue Patty and Thomas. The yearnings of his heart told him that a few hours' delay might be fatal to his children. Meantime, the first relief, with their little company, now reduced to nineteen, passed forward toward the settlements. At Bear Valley, another cache of provisions had been made, and this was found unmolested. Camping at this place, the utmost precaution was taken to prevent the poor starved people from over-eating. After a sufficient quantity of food was distributed, the remainder of the provisions was hung up in a tree. Of course, the small portion distributed to each did not satisfy the cravings of hunger. Sometime during the night, Wm. Hook quietly crept to the tree, climbed up to the food, and ate until his hunger was appeased. Poor boy; it was a fatal act. Toward morning it was discovered that he was dying. All that the company could do to relieve his sufferings was done, but it was of no avail. Finding that the poor boy was past relief, most of the emigrants moved on toward the settlements. Wm. G. Murphy's feet had been badly frozen, and he was suffering such excruciating agony that he could not travel and keep up with the others. At his request, his sister Mary had cut his shoes open in order to get them off, and his feet thereupon swelled up as if they had been scalded. Because he could not walk, the company left him with William Hook. A camp-keeper also remained. This boy's death is thus described by Mr. Murphy, who writes :

" William Hook went out on the snow and rested on his knees and elbows. The camp-keeper called to him to come in. He then told me to make him come into camp. I went and put my hand on him, speaking his name, and he fell over, being already dead. He did not die in great agony, as is usually alleged. No groan, nor signs of dying, were manifested to us. The camp-keeper and myself took the biscuits and jerked beef from his pockets, and buried him just barely under the ground, near a tree which had been fired, and from around which the snow had melted." Those who were in the company thought Wm. G. Murphy could not possibly walk, but when all had gone, and Hook was dead, and no alternative remained but to walk or die, he did walk. It took him two days to go bare-footed over the snow to Mule Springs, a journey which the others had made in one day. The agony which he endured during that trip can better be imagined than described. Nothing but an indom-itable will could ever have sustained him during those two days.

All the members of this relief party suffered greatly, and several came near perishing. Little James F. Reed, Jr., was too small to step in the tracks made by the older members of the party. In order to travel with the rest he had to partly use his knees in walking. When one foot was in a track he would place the other knee on the untrodden snow, and was thus enabled to put his foot in the next track. John Denton was left with a good fire, and when last seen was reclining smoking, on a bed of freshly gathered pine boughs. He looked so comfortable that the little timid boy James, begged hard to be allowed to remain with him. Mrs. Reed had hard work to coax him to come. Among other things she promised that when he reached California, he should have a horse "all for himself," and that he should never have to walk any more. This promise was literally fulfilled. Jas. F. Reed, Jr., after reaching California, always had a horse of his own. No matter what vicissitudes of fortune over-took him, he has always kept a saddle horse.

Sad scenes were occurring at the cabin at Donner Lake and Alder Creek. Starvation was fast claiming its victims. The poor sufferers tried to be brave and trust God, but sometimes hope well-nigh dis-appeared. The evening prayers were always read in Patrick Breen's cabin, and all the inmates knelt and joined in the responses. Once when they were thus praying, they heard the cries of wild geese flying over the cabin. With one accord all raised their heads and listened for a moment to the soul-inspiring sound. "Thank God, the Spring is coming," was all Patrick Breen said, and again bowing their heads the prayer was resumed.

Charles L. Cady, writing from Calistoga, says, that Commodore Stockton employed Greenwood and Turner to guide the second relief party over the mountains to Donner Lake. After meeting the first relief, and the emigrants whom they had in charge, there was no longer any need for the guides, because the plain beaten path in the snow could be readily followed. Cady, Stone, and Clark, being young, vigorous men, left their companions, or were sent forward by Reed, and reached the cabins some hours in advance of the party.

In Patrick Breen's diary is found the following:

" Feb. 23. Froze hard last night. To day pleasant and thawy ; has the appearance of Spring, all but the deep snow. Wind south-south-east. Shot a dog to-day and dressed his flesh.

" Feb. 25. To-day Mrs. Murphy says the wolves are about to dig up the dead bodies around her shanty, and the nights are too cold to watch them, but we hear them howl.

" Feb. 26. Hungry times in camp ; plenty of hides, but the folks will not eat them ; we eat them with tolerably good appetite, thanks to the Almighty God. Mrs. Murphy said here yesterday that she thought she would commence on Milton and eat him. I do not think she has done so yet ; it is distressing. The Donners told the California folks four days ago that they would commence on the dead people if they did not succeed that day or the next in finding their cattle, then ten or twelve feet under the snow, and did not know the spot, or near it ; they have done it ere this.

" Feb. 28. One solitary Indian passed by yesterday ; came from the lake ; had a heavy pack on his back ; gave me five or six roots resembling onions in shape ; tasted some like a sweet potato ; full of tough little fibers.

" March 1. Ten men arrived this morning from Bear Valley, with provisions. We are to start in two or three days, and cache our goods here. They say the snow will remain until June."

This closes Patrick Breen's diary. Its record has always been considered reliable. None of the statements made in this diary have ever been controverted.

The Indian spoken of refused to be interviewed. To quote the language of Mr. John Breen, " He did not seem to be at all curious as to how or why there was a white man alone (as it must have

seemed to him) in the wilderness of snow." The Indian was trudging along with a heavy pack on his back. As soon as he saw Mr.
Breen, he halted and warned him with a gesture not to approach.
Taking from the pack a few of the fibrous roots, he laid them on the
snow, still cautioning with his hand not to approach until he was
well out of reach. As soon as the Indian was gone, Mr. Breen went
out and got the roots, which were very palatable.

When Patty and Thomas Reed had been returned to the cabins
by Aquilla Glover, they had been received by the Breen family.
The Breen cabin was the first one at which Mr. Reed arrived. His
meeting with his daughter is thus described by Mr. Eddy, in Thornton's work: "At this camp Mr. Reed saw his daughter Patty sitting
on the top of the snow with which the cabin was covered. Patty
saw her father at some distance, and immediately started to run and
meet him, but such was her weakness that she fell. Her father took
her up, and the affectionate girl, bathed in tears, embraced and kissed
him, exclaiming: 'Oh, papa! I never expected to see you again
when the cruel people drove you out of camp. But I knew that
God was good, and would do what was best. Is dear mamma
living? Is Mr. Glover living? Did you know that he was a
Mason? Oh, my dear papa, I am so hapyy to see you. Masons
must be good men. Is Mr. Glover the same sort of Mason we had
in Springfield? He promised mamma upon the word of a Mason
that he would bring me and Tommy out of the mountains.' Mr.
Reed told Patty that Masons were everywhere the same, and that he
had met her mother and Mr. Glover, and had relieved him from his
pledge, and that he himself had come to her and little Tommy to
redeem that pledge and to take out all that were able to travel."

The greatest precaution was taken to keep the suffering emigrants
from over-eating. Cady, Stone and Clark, who went ahead, had
distributed a small portion of food to each of the famished beings.
Patty Reed was entrusted with the task of giving to each person a
single biscuit. Taking the biscuits in her apron she went in turn to
each member of the company. Who shall describe the rejoicings
that were held over those biscuits? Several of the survivors, in

speaking of the subject, say that to their hungry eyes these small pieces of bread assumed gigantic proportions.   Never did the largest loaves of bread look half so large.   Patty Reed says that some of the little girls cut their portions into thin slices, so as to eat them slowly and enjoy them more completely.

The names of the members of this second relief party, were James F. Reed, Charles Cady, Charles Stone, —— Clark, Joseph Jondro, Mathew Dofar, John Turner, Hiram Miller, Wm. McCutchen and Brit. Greenwood.   A portion of the party went to the Donner tents, and the remainder assisted the emigrants in preparing to start over the mountains.   The distress and suffering at each camp was extreme. The following, taken from Thornton's work, vividly illustrates one picture presented to the eyes of the second relief party :

"After giving some bread to his own and Mr. Breen's children, Mr. Reed went to Keseberg's cabin, where he found Mr. Stone, who had given them some refreshments and was washing the children's clothes.   He found them in a most deplorable condition.   Mr. Foster's child and Mr. Reed's were in bed, crying incessantly for something to eat.   They would stretch out their arms and beg in the most moving terms for food.   Mr. Stone had already given the children all that he prudently could ; but such was the force of the affecting appeal made by these poor, helpless and unprotected suffer-ers, that Mr. Reed could not restrain the promptings of his Irish heart or refrain from giving heed to their cries, and he gave them more, perhaps, than was prudent.   Mrs. Murphy, an amiable woman and the grandmother of Mr. Foster's children, informed Mr. Reed that these children had been in that bed fourteen days.   The imagination must fill up the picture."

The threatening appearance of the weather, and the short supply of provisions on hand, urged Mr. Reed and his party to return as speedily as possible.   Those who started from Donner Lake with Mr. Reed and his party, were Patrick Breen, Mrs. Margaret Breen, John Breen, Patrick Breen, Jr., James F. Breen, Peter Breen and Isabella M. Breen, Patty Reed and Thomas Reed, Isaac Donner and Mary M. Donner, Solomon Hook, Mrs. Elizabeth Graves, Nancy

Graves, Jonathan Graves, Franklin Graves and Elizabeth Graves, Jr.
Many of the younger members of this party had to be carried. All
were very much weakened and emaciated, and it was evident that
the journey over the mountains would be slow and painful.   In case
a storm should occur on the summits, it was fearfully apparent that
the trip would be exceedingly perilous.

Mrs. Tamsen Donner still determined to remain with her invalid
husband, though urgently entreated to save her life by joining this
party.   Clark, Cady and Stone, were left at the Donner tents at
Alder Creek, when the remainder of the relief party started for the
settlements.   These men were induced by Mrs. Tamsen Donner to
attempt to rescue her three youngest daughters, Frances, Georgia,
and Eliza.   They took the children as far as the cabins at the lake,
and left them.   Probably they were frightened at the storm which
they saw gathering over the summit.   In view of the terrible calamity
which befell the party on account of this storm, no one can blame
the men for their action in leaving the children at the cabins.   The
parting between the devoted mother and her little ones is thus briefly
described by Georgia Donner, now Mrs. Babcock : "Cady, Stone and
Clark came.   I listened to their talking as they made their agreement.
Then they took us, three little girls, up the snow steps, and stood us
on the bank.   Mother came, put on our hoods and cloaks, saying, as
if she was talking more to herself than to us, ' I may never see you
again, but God will take care of you.'   After traveling a few miles
they left us on the snow, went ahead a short distance, talked to one
another, then came back, took us as far as Keseberg's cabin, and
left us."

Mr. Cady recalls the incident of leaving the children on the snow,
but says the party saw a coyote, and were attempting to get a shot
at the animal.

Reed's party encamped the first night near the upper end of Donner Lake.   They had scarcely traveled three miles.   Upon starting
from the Graves cabin, Mrs. Graves had taken with her a considerable sum of money.   This money, Mr. McCutchen says, had been
ingeniously concealed in auger holes bored in cleats nailed to the

bed of the wagon. These cleats, as W. C. Graves informs us, were ostensibly placed in the wagon bed to support a table carried in the back part of the wagon. On the under side of these cleats, however, were the auger-holes carefully filled with coin. The sum is variously stated at from three to five hundred dollars. At the camping-ground near the upper end of Donner Lake, one of the relief party jokingly proposed to another to play a game of euchre to see who should have Mrs. Graves' money. The next morning Mrs. Graves remained behind when the party started, and concealed her money. All that is known is, that she buried it behind a large rock on the north side of Donner Lake. So far as is known, this money has never been recovered, but still lies hidden where it was placed by Mrs. Graves.

Chapter XIV.

CLARK, Stone, and Cady remained at the mountain camps when the second relief started over the mountains. It was intended that these men should attend to procuring wood and do such other acts as would assist the almost helpless sufferers. It was thought that a third relief party could be sent out in a few days to get all the emigrants who remained. Clark did stay until the third relief arrived, but Cady and Stone, finding the provisions nearly exhausted, and knowing that a storm was imminent, attempted to follow Reed and his companions. As will presently be seen, this came near being a fatal undertaking.

When the second relief party and the little band of famished emigrants had traveled three days, they found themselves on the evening of the third in a cold, bleak, uncomfortable hollow, somewhere near the lower end of Summit Valley. Here, the storm which had been brewing for some days past, broke in all its fury upon the doomed company. In addition to the cold, sleet-like snow, a fierce, penetrating wind seemed to freeze the very marrow in their bones. The relief party had urged the tired, hungry, enfeebled emigrants forward at the greatest possible speed all day, in order to get as near the settlements as they could before the storm should burst upon them. Besides, their provisions were exhausted, and they were anxious to reach certain caches of supplies which they had made while going to the cabins. Fearing that the storm would prevent the party from reaching these caches, Mr. Reed sent Joseph Jondro, Matthew Dofar, and Hiram Turner forward to the first cache, with instructions to get the provisions and return to the suffering emigrants. That very night the storm came, and the three men had not been heard from.

The camp was in a most inhospitable spot. Exposed to the fury of the wind and storm, shelterless, supperless, overwhelmed with discouragements, the entire party sank down exhausted upon the snow. The entire party? No! There was one man who never ceased to work. When a fire had been kindled, and nearly every one had given up, this one man, unaided, continued to strive to erect some sort of shelter to protect the defenseless women and children. Planting large pine boughs in the snow, he banked up the snow on either side of them so as to form a wall. Hour after hour, in the darkness and raging storm, he toiled on alone, building the sheltering breastwork which was to ward off death from the party who by this time had crept shiveringly under its protection. But for this shelter all would have perished before morning. At midnight the man was still at work. The darting snow particles seemed to cut his eye-balls, and the glare of the fire, and the great physical exhaustion under which he was laboring, gradually rendered him blind. Like his companions, he had borne a child in his arms all day over the soft, yielding snow. Like them he was drenched to the skin, and his clothing was frozen stiff and hard with ice. Yet he kept up the fire, built a great sheltering wall about the sufferers, and went here and there amongst the wailing and dying. With unabated violence the storm continued its relentless fury. The survivors say it was the coldest night they ever experienced. There is a limit to human endurance. The man was getting stone blind. Had he attempted to speak, his tongue would have cloven to the roof of his mouth. His senses were chilled, blunted, dead. Sleep had stilled the plaintive cries of those about him. All was silent save the storm. Without knowing it, this heroic man was yielding to a sleep more powerful than that which had overcome his companions. While trying to save those who were weaker than himself, he had been literally freezing. Sightless, benumbed, moving half unconsciously about his work, he staggered, staggered, staggered, and finally sank in the snow. All slept! As he put no more fuel upon the fire, the flames died down. The logs upon which the fire had rested gave way, and most of the coals fell upon the snow. They were in almost total darkness.

Presently some one awoke. It was Mrs. Breen, whose motherly watchfulness prevented more than a few consecutive moments' sleep. The camp was quickly aroused. All were nearly frozen. Hiram Miller's hands were so cold and frosted, that the skin on the fingers cracked open when he tried to split some kindlings. At last the fire was somehow renewed. Meantime they had discovered their leader—he who had been working throughout the night—lying cold, speechless and apparently dead upon the snow. Hiram Miller and Wm. McCutchen carried the man to the fire, chafed his hands and limbs, rubbed his body vigorously, and worked with him as hard as they could for two hours before he showed signs of returning consciousness. Redoubling their exertions, they kept at work until the cold, gray morning dawned, ere the man was fully restored. Would you know the name of this man, this hero? It was James Frazier Reed.

From this time forward, all the toil, all the responsibility devolved upon Wm. McCutchen and Hiram Miller. Jondro, Dofar and Turner, were caught in the drifts ahead. The fishers or other wild animals had almost completely devoured the first cache of provisions, and while these men were trying to reach the second cache, the storm imprisoned them. They could neither go forward nor return. Cady and Stone were between Donner Lake and Starved Camp, and were in a like helpless condition. McCutchen and Miller were the only ones able to do anything toward saving the poor creatures who were huddled together at the miserable camp. All the other men were completely disheartened by the fearful calamity which had overtaken them. But for the untiring exertions of these two men, death to all would have been certain. McCutchen had on four shirts, and yet he became so chilled while trying to kindle the fire, that in getting warm he burned the back out of his shirts. He only discovered the mishap by the scorching and burning of his flesh.

What a picture of desolation was presented to the inmates of the Starved Camp during the next three days. It stormed incessantly. One who has not witnessed a storm on the Sierras cannot imagine the situation. A quotation from Bret Harte's Gabriel Conroy will afford the best idea of the situation:

"Snow. Everywhere. As far as the eye could reach—fifty miles, looking southward from the highest white peak. Filling ravines and gulches, and dropping from the walls of canyons in white shroud-like drifts, fashioning the dividing ridge into the likeness of a monstrous grave, hiding the bases of giant pines, and completely covering young trees and larches, rimming with porcelain the bowl-like edges of still, cold lakes, and undulating in motionless white billows to the edge of the distant horizon. Snow lying everywhere on the California Sierras, and still falling. It had been snowing in finely, granulated powder, in damp, spongy flakes, in thin feathery plumes; snowing from a leaden sky steadily, snowing fiercely, shaken out of purple-black clouds in white flocculent masses, or dropping in long level lines like white lances from the tumbled and broken heavens. But always silently! The woods were so choked with it, it had so cushioned and muffled the ringing rocks and echoing hills, that all sound was deadened. The strongest gust, the fiercest blast, awoke no sigh or complaint from the snow-packed, rigid files of forest. There was no cracking of bough nor crackle of underbrush; the overladen branches of pine and fir yielded and gave away without a sound. The silence was vast, measureless, complete !"

Death entered the camp on the first night. He came to claim one who was a true, faithful mother. One who merits more fitting praise than pen can give. Though comparatively little has been

9

told concerning her life by the survivors, doubt not that Mrs. Eliza-beth Graves was one of the noblest of the mothers of the Donner Party. Her charity is kindly remembered by all who have spoken her name. To her companions in misfortune she always gave such food as she possessed; for her children she now gave her life. The last morsels of food, the last grain of flour, she had placed in the mouths of her babes, though she was dying of starvation.

Mrs. Farnham, who talked personally with Mrs. Breen, gives the following description of that terrible night:

"Mrs. Breen told me that she had her husband and five children together, lying with their feet to the fire, and their heads under shelter of the snow breast-work. She sat by them, with only mocca-sins on her feet, and a blanket drawn over her shoulders and head, within which, and a shawl she constantly wore, she nursed her poor baby on her knees. Her milk had been gone several days, and the child was so emaciated and lifeless that she scarcely expected at any time on opening the covering to find it alive. Mrs. Graves lay with her babe and three or four older children at the other side of the fire. The storm was very violent all night, and she watched through it, dozing occasionally for a few minutes, and then rousing herself to brush the snow and flying sparks from the covering of the sleepers. Toward morning she heard one of the young girls opposite call to her mother to cover her. The call was repeated several times impa-tiently, when she spoke to the child, reminding her of the exhaustion and fatigue her mother suffered in nursing and carrying the baby, and bidding her cover herself, and let her mother rest. Presently she heard the mother speak, in a quiet, unnatural tone, and she called to one of the men near her to go and speak to her. He arose after a few minutes, and found the poor sufferer almost past speak-ing. He took her infant, and after shaking the snow from her blanket, covered her as well as might be. Shortly after, Mrs. Breen observed her to turn herself slightly, and throw one arm feebly up, as if to go to sleep. She waited a little while, and seeing her remain quite still, she walked around to her. She was already cold in death. Her poor starving child wailed and moaned piteously in the arms of its young sister, but the mother's heart could no more warm or nourish it."

The members of the second relief party realized that they were themselves in imminent danger of death. They were powerless to carry the starving children over the deep, soft, fresh fallen snow, and it was doubtful if they would be able to reach the settlements unincumbered. Isaac Donner, one of the sons of Jacob and Elizabeth Donner, perished during one of the stormy nights. He was lying on the bed of pine boughs between his sister Mary and Patty Reed, and died so quietly that neither of the sleeping girls awoke.

The relief party determined to set out over the snow, hasten to the settlements, and send back relief. Solomon Hook, Jacob Donner's oldest boy, insisted that he was able to walk, and therefore joined the party. Hiram Miller, an old friend of the Reed family, took little Thomas Reed in his arms, and set out with the others. Patty Reed, full of hope and courage, refused to be carried by her father, and started on foot.

With what emotions did the poor sufferers in Starved Camp watch the party as it disappeared among the pines! There was no food in camp, and death had already selected two of their number. What a pitiable group it was! Could a situation more desolate or deplorable be imagined? Mr. Breen, as has been heretofore mentioned, was feeble, sickly, and almost as helpless as the children. Upon Mrs. Breen devolved the care, not only of her husband, but of all who remained in the fatal camp, for all others were children. John Breen, their eldest son, was the strongest and most vigorous in the family, yet the following incident shows how near he was to death's door. It must have occurred the morning the relief party left. The heat of the fire had melted a deep round hole in the snow. At the bottom of the pit was the fire. The men were able to descend the sides of this cavity, and frequently did so to attend to the fire. At one time, while William McCutchen was down by the fire, John Breen was sitting on the end of one of the logs on which the fire had originally been kindled. Several logs had been laid side by side, and the fire had been built in the middle of the floor thus constructed. While the central logs had burned out and let the fire descend, the outer logs remained with their ends on the firm snow. On one of these logs John Breen was sitting. Suddenly overcome by fatigue and hunger, he fainted and dropped headlong into the fire-pit. Fortunately, Mr. McCutchen caught the falling boy, and thus saved him from a horrible death. It was some time before the boy was fully restored to consciousness. Mrs. Breen had a small quantity of sugar, and a little was placed between his clenched teeth. This seemed to revive him, and he not only survived, but is living to-day, the head of a large family, in San Benito County.

Mrs. Breen's younger children, Patrick, James, Peter, and the nursing babe, Isabella, were completely helpless and dependent. Not less helpless were the orphan children of Mr. and Mrs. Graves. Nancy was only about nine years old, and upon her devolved the task of caring for the babe, Elizabeth. Nancy Graves is now the wife of the earnest and eloquent divine, Rev. R. W. Williamson, of Los Gatos, Santa Clara County. To her lasting honor be it said, that although she was dying of hunger in Starved Camp, yet she faithfully tended, cared for, and saved her baby sister. Aside from occasional bits of sugar, this baby and Mrs. Breen's had nothing for an entire week, save snow-water. Besides Nancy and Elizabeth, there were of the Graves children, Jonathan, aged seven, and Franklin, aged five years. Franklin soon perished. Starvation and exposure had so reduced his tiny frame, that he could not endure these days of continual fasting.

Mary M. Donner, whom all mention as one of the most lovely girls in the Donner Party, met with a cruel accident the night before the relief party left Starved Camp. Her feet had become frozen and insensible to pain. Happening to lie too near the fire, one of her feet became dreadfully burned. She suffered excruciating agony, yet evinced remarkable fortitude. She ultimately lost four toes from her left foot, on account of this sad occurrence.

Seven of the Breens, Mary Donner, and the three children of Mr. and Mrs. Graves, made the eleven now waiting for relief at Starved Camp. Mrs. Graves, her child Franklin, and the boy, Isaac Donner, who lay stark in death upon the snow, completed the fourteen who were left by the relief party.

Meantime, how fared it with those who were pressing forward toward the settlements? At each step they sank two or three feet into the snow. Of course those who were ahead broke the path, and the others, as far as possible, stepped in their tracks. This, Patty Reed could not do, because she was too small. So determined was she, however, that despite the extra exertion she was compelled to undergo, she would not admit being either cold or fatigued. Patty Reed has been mentioned as only eight years old. Many of the survivors speak of her, however, in much the same terms as John Breen, who says: " I was under the impression that she was older. She had a wonderful mind for one of her age. She had, I have often thought, as much sense as a grown person." Over Patty's large dark eyes, on this morning, gradually crept a film. Previous starvation had greatly attenuated her system, and she was far too weak to endure the hardship she had undertaken. Gradually the snow-mantled forests, the forbidding mountains, the deep, dark canyon of Bear River, and even the forms of her companions, faded from view. In their stead came a picture of such glory and brightness as seldom comes to human eyes. It was a vision of angels and of brilliant stars. She commenced calling her father, and those with him, and began talking about the radiant forms that hovered over her. Her wan, pale face was illumined with smiles, and with an ecstasy of joy she talked of the angels and stars, and of the happiness she experienced. "Why, Reed," exclaimed McCutchen, "Patty is dying!" And it was too true.

For a few moments the party forgot their own sufferings and trials, and ministered to the wants of the spirituelle child, whose entrance into the dark valley had been heralded by troops of white-winged angels. At the Starved Camp Reed had taken the hard, frozen sacks in which the provisions had been carried, and by holding them to the fire, had thawed out the seams, and scraped therefrom about a teaspoonful of crumbs. These he had placed in the thumb of his woolen mitten to be used in case of emergency. Little did he suppose that the emergency would come so soon. Warming and moistening these crumbs between his own lips, the father placed them in his child's mouth. Meantime they had wrapped a blanket around her chilled form, and were busily chafing her hands and feet. Her first return to consciousness was signalled by the regrets she expressed at having been awakened from her beautiful dream. To this day she cherishes the memory of that vision as the dearest, most enchanting of all her life. After this some of the kind-hearted Frenchmen in the party took turns with Reed in carrying Patty upon their backs.

Past-midshipman S. E. Woodworth is a name that figures conspicuously among the relief parties organized to rescue the Donner Party. At the time Reed and his companions were suffering untold horrors on the mountains, and those left at Starved Camp were perishing of starvation, Woodworth, with an abundance of supplies, was lying idle in camp at Bear Valley.

The three men who had been sent forward to the caches, left the remnant of the provisions which had not been destroyed, where it could easily be seen by Reed and his companions. Hurrying forward, they reached Woodworth's camp, and two men, John Stark and Howard Oakley, returned and met Reed's party. It was quite time. With frozen feet, and exhausted bodies, the members of the second relief were in a sad plight. They left the settlements strong, hearty men. They returned in a half-dead condition. Several lost some of their toes on account of having them frozen, and one or two were crippled for life. They had been three days on the way from Starved Camp to Woodworth's. Cady and Stone overtook Reed and his companions on the second day after leaving Starved Camp. On the night of the third day, they reached Woodworth's.

When Patty Reed reached Woodworth's, and had been provided with suitable food, an incident occurred which fully illustrates the tenderness and womanliness of her nature. Knowing that her mother and dear ones were safe; knowing that relief would speedily return to those on the mountains; realizing that for her there was to be no more hunger, or snow, and that she would no longer be separated from her father, her feelings may well be imagined. In her quiet joy she was not wholly alone. Hidden away in her bosom, during all the suffering and agony of the journey over the mountains, were a number of childish treasures. First, there was a lock of silvery gray hair which her own hand had cut from the head of her Grandmother Keyes way back on the Big Blue River. Patty had always been a favorite of her grandma, and when the latter died, Patty secured this lock of hair. She tied it up in a little piece of old-fashioned lawn, dotted with wee blue flowers, and always had carried it in her bosom. But this was not all. She had a dainty little glass salt-cellar, scarcely larger than the inside of a humming bird's nest, and what was more precious than this, a tiny wooden doll. This doll had been her constant companion. It had black eyes and hair, and was indeed very pretty. At Woodworth's camp, Patty told "Dolly" all her joy and gladness, and who cannot pardon the little girl for thinking her dolly looked happy as she listened.

Patty Reed is now Mrs. Frank Lewis, of San Jose, Cal. She has a pleasant home and a beautiful family of children. Yet oftentimes the mother, the grown up daughters, and the younger members of the family, gather with tear-dimmed eyes about a little sacred box. In this box is the lock of hair in the piece of lawn, the tiny salt-cellar, the much loved "Dolly," and an old woolen mitten, in the thumb of which are yet the traces of fine crumbs.

CHAPTER XV

RS. MARGARET BREEN performed a noble part in this
Donner tragedy, which part has been beautifully recorded
by a woman's hand. It is written so tenderly, so deli-
cately, and with so much reverence for the maternal love
which alone sustained Mrs. Breen, that it can hardly be
improved. This account was published by its author,
Mrs. Farnham, in 1849, and is made the basis of the following
sketch. With alterations here and there, made for the sake of brev-
ity, the article is as it was written:

There was no food in Starved Camp. There was nothing to eat
save a few seeds, tied in bits of cloth, that had been brought along
by some one, and the precious lump of sugar. There were also a
few teaspoonfuls of tea. They sat and lay by the fire most of the
day, with what heavy hearts, who shall know. They were upon
about thirty feet of snow. The dead lay before them, a ghastlier
sight in the sunshine that succeeded the storm, than when the dark
clouds overhung them. They had no words of cheer to speak to
each other—no courage or hope to share—but those which pointed

to a life where hunger and cold could never come, and their benumbed faculties were scarcely able to seize upon a consolation so
remote from the thoughts and wants that absorbed their whole being.

A situation like this will not awaken in common natures religious
trust. Under such protracted suffering, the animal outgrows the
spiritual in frightful disproportion. Yet the mother's sublime faith,
which had brought her thus far through her agonies, with a heart
still warm toward those who shared them, did not fail her now.
She spoke gently to one and another. Asked her husband to repeat
the Litany, and the children to join her in the responses; and endeavored to fix their minds upon the time when the relief would
probably come. Nature, as unerringly as philosophy could have
done, taught her that the only hope of sustaining those about her,
was to set before them a termination to their sufferings.

What days and nights were those that went by while they waited.
Life waning visibly in those about her; not a morsel of food to offer
them; her own infant—and the little one that had been cherished
and saved through all by the mother now dead— wasting hourly into
the more perfect image of death; her husband worn to a skeleton;
it needed the fullest measure of exalted faith, of womanly tenderness
and self-sacrifice, to sustain her through such a season. She watched
by night as well as by day. She gathered wood to keep them warm.
She boiled the handful of tea and dispensed it to them, and when
she found one sunken and speechless, she broke with her teeth a
morsel of the precious sugar, and put it in his lips. She fed her
babe freely on snow water, and scanty as was the wardrobe she had,
she managed to get fresh clothing next to its skin two or three times
a week. Where, one asks in wonder and reverence, did she get the
strength and courage for all of this? She sat all night by her family,
her elbows on her knees, brooding over the meek little victim that
lay there, watching those who slept, and occasionally dozing with a
fearful consciousness of their terrible condition always upon her.
The sense of peril never slumbered. Many times during the night
she went to the sleepers to ascertain if they all still breathed. She
put her hand under their blankets, and held it before the mouth.

In this way she assured herself that they were yet alive. But once
her blood curdled to find, on approaching her hand to the lips of
one of her own children, there was no warm breath upon it. She
tried to open the mouth, and found the jaws set. She roused her
husband, "Oh! Patrick, man! arise and help me! James is dying!"
"Let him die!" said the miserable father, "he will be better off
than any of us." She was terribly shocked by this reply. In her
own expressive language, her heart stood still when she heard it.
She was bewildered and knew not where to set her weary hands to
work, but she recovered in a few moments and began to chafe the
breast and hands of the perishing boy. She broke a bit of sugar,
and with considerable effort forced it between his teeth with a few
drops of snow water. She saw him swallow, then a slight convulsive
motion stirred his features, he stretched his limbs feebly, and in a
moment more opened his eyes and looked upon her. How fervent
were her thanks to the Great Father whom she forgot not day or
night.

Thus she went on. The tea leaves were eaten, the seeds chewed,
the sugar all dispensed. The days were bright, and compared with
the nights, comfortable. Occasionally when the sun shone their
voices were heard, though generally they sat or laid in a kind of
stupor from which she often found it alarmingly difficult to arouse
them. When the gray evening twilight drew its deepening curtain
over the cold glittering heavens and the icy waste, and when the
famishing bodies had been covered from the frost that pinched them
with but little less keenness than the unrelenting hunger, the solitude
seemed to rend her very brain. Her own powers faltered. But she
said her prayers over many times in the darkness as well as the light,
and always with renewed trust in Him who had not yet forsaken her,
and thus she sat out her weary watch. After the turning of the
night she always sat watching for the morning star, which seemed
every time she saw it rise clear in the cold eastern sky, to renew the
promise, "As thy day is, so shall thy strength be."

Their fire had melted the snow to a considerable depth, and they
were lying on the bank above. Thus they had less of its heat than

they needed, and found some difficulty in getting the fuel she gathered, placed so it would burn. One morning, after she had hailed her messenger of promise, and the light had increased so as to render objects visible in the distance, she looked as usual over the white expanse that lay to the southwest, to see if any dark moving specks were visible upon its surface. Only the tree-tops which she had scanned so often as to be quite familiar with their appearance, were to be seen. With a heavy heart she brought herself back from that distant hope to consider what was immediately about her. The fire had sunk so far away, that they had felt but little of its warmth the last two nights, and casting her eyes down into the snow-pit, whence it sent forth only a dull glow, she thought she saw the welcome face of beloved mother Earth. It was such a renewing sight after their long, freezing separation from it! She immediately aroused her eldest son, John, and with a great deal of difficulty, and repeated words of cheering and encouragement, brought him to understand that she wished him to descend by one of the tree-tops which had fallen in so as to make a sort of ladder, and see if they could reach the naked earth, and if it were possible for them all to go down. She trembled with fear at the vacant silence in which he at first gazed at her, but at length, after she had told him a great many times, he said "Yes, mother," and went.

He reached the bottom safely, and presently spoke to her. There was naked, dry earth under his feet; it was warm, and he wished her to come down. She laid her baby beside some of the sleepers, and descended. Immediately she determined upon taking them all down. How good, she thought as she descended the boughs, was the God whom she trusted. By perseverance, by entreaty, by encouragement, and with her own aid, she got them into this snug shelter.

Relief came not, and as starvation crept closer and closer to himself and those about him, Patrick Breen determined that it was his duty to employ the means of sustaining life which God seemed to have placed before them. The lives of all might be saved by resorting to such food as others, in like circumstances, had subsisted upon.

Mrs. Breen, however, declared that she would die, or see her children die, before her life or theirs should be preserved by such means.   If ever the father gave to the dying children, it was without her consent or knowledge.   She never tasted, nor knew of her children partaking.   Mrs. Farnham says that when Patrick Breen ascended to obtain the dreadful repast, his wife, frozen with horror, hid her face in her hands, and could not look up.   She was conscious of his return, and of something going on about the fire, but she could not bring herself to uncover her eyes till all had subsided again into silence.   Her husband remarked that perhaps they were wrong in rejecting a means of sustaining life of which others had availed themselves, but she put away the suggestion so fearfully that it was never renewed, nor acted upon by any of her family.   She and her children were now, indeed, reaching the utmost verge of life. A little more battle with the grim enemies that had pursued them so relentlessly, twenty-four, or at most forty-eight hours of such warfare, and all would be ended.   The infants still breathed, but were so wasted they could only be moved by raising them bodily with the hands.   It seemed as if even their light weight would have dragged the limbs from their bodies.   Occasionally, through the day, she ascended the tree to look out.   It was an incident now, and seemed to kindle more life than when it only required a turn of the head or a glance of the eye to tell that there was no living thing near them. She could no longer walk on the snow, but she had still strength enough to crawl from tree to tree and gather a few boughs which she threw along before her to the pit, and piled them in to renew the fire. The eighth day was passed.   On the ninth morning she ascended to watch for her star of mercy.   Clear and bright it stood over against her beseeching gaze, set in the light liquid blue that overflows the pathway of the opening day.   She prayed earnestly as she gazed, for she knew that there were but few hours of life in those dearest to her.   If human aid came not that day, some eyes, that would soon look imploringly into hers, would be closed in death before that star would rise again.   Would she herself, with all her endurance and resisting love, live to see it?   Were they at length to perish?   Great

God! should it be permitted that they who had been preserved through so much, should die at last so miserably?

Her eyes were dim, and her sight wavering. She could not distinguish trees from men on the snow, but had they been near, she could have heard them, for her ear had grown so sensitive that the slightest unaccustomed noise arrested her attention. She went below with a heavier heart than ever before. She had not a word of hope to answer the languid inquiring countenances that were turned to her face, and she was conscious that it told the story of her despair. Yet she strove with some half insane words to suggest that somebody would surely come to them that day. Another would be too late, and the pity of men's hearts and the mercy of God would surely bring them. The pallor of death seemed already to be stealing over the sunken countenances that surrounded her, and weak as she was, she could remain below but a few minutes together. She felt she could have died had she let go her resolution at any time within the last forty-eight hours. They repeated the Litany. The responses came so feebly that they were scarcely audible, and the protracted utterances seemed wearisome. At last it was over, and they rested in silence.

The sun mounted high and higher in the heavens, and when the day was three or four hours old she placed her trembling feet again upon the ladder to look out once more. The corpses of the dead lay always before her as she reached the top—the mother and her son, and the little boy, whose remains she could not even glance at since they had been mutilated. The blanket that covered them could not shut out the horror of the sight.

The rays of the sun fell on her with a friendly warmth, but she could not look into the light that flooded the white expanse. Her eyes lacked strength and steadiness, and she rested herself against a tree and endeavored to gather her wandering faculties in vain. The enfeebled will could no longer hold rule over them. She had broken perceptions, fragments of visions, contradictory and mixed—former mingled with latter times. Recollections of plenty and rural peace came up from her clear tranquil childhood, which seemed to have been another state of existence; flashes of her latter life—its comfort and abundance—gleams of maternal pride in her children who had been growing up about her to ease and independence.

She lived through all the phases which her simple life had ever worn, in the few moments of repose after the dizzy effort of ascending; as the thin blood left her whirling brain and returned to its shrunken channels, she grew more clearly conscious of the terrible present, and remembered the weary quest upon which she came. It was not the memory of thought, it was that of love, the old tugging at the heart that had never relaxed long enough to say: "Now I am done; I can bear no more!" The miserable ones down there—for them her wavering life came back; at thought of them she turned her face listlessly the way it had so often gazed. But this time, something caused it to flush as if the blood, thin and cold as it was, would burst its vessels! What was it? Nothing that she saw, for her eyes were quite dimmed by the sudden access of excitement! It was the sound of voices! By a superhuman effort she kept herself from falling! Was it reality or delusion? She must at least live to know the truth. It came again and again. She grew calmer as she became more assured, and the first distinct words she heard uttered were, "There is Mrs. Breen alive yet, anyhow!" Three men were advancing toward her. She knew that now there would be no more starving. Death was repelled for this time from the precious little flock he had so long threatened, and she might offer up thanksgiving unchecked by the dreads and fears that had so long frozen her.

Chapter XVI.

OHN STARK, Howard Oakley and Charles Stone were the three men who were approaching Starved Camp. These men form a portion of the third relief party. At the time Reed's party was approaching Woodworth's camp at Bear Valley, Wm. M. Foster and W. H. Eddy were approaching the same camp from the opposite direction. Foster and Eddy, it will be remembered, were of the fifteen who composed the Forlorn Hope. Foster was a man of strong, generous impulses, and great determination. His boy was at Donner Lake, and his wife's mother and brother. He hardly took time to rest and recruit his wasted strength before he began organizing a party to go to their rescue. His efforts were ably seconded by W. H. Eddy, whose wife and daughter had perished, but whose boy was still alive at the cabins.

California was thoroughly aroused over tidings which had come from the mountains. It was difficult to get volunteers to undertake the journey over the Sierras, but horses, mules, provisions and good wages were allowed all who would venture the perilous trip. The trouble with Mexico had caused many of the able-bodied citizens of

California to enlist in the service. Hence it was that it was so difficult to organize relief parties.

The following extracts are made from the California Star, a newspaper published at "Yerba Buena," as San Francisco was then called. They do justice to the sentiment of the people of California, and indicate something of the willingness of the pioneers to aid the Donner Party. From the Star of January 16th, 1847, is taken the following article, which appeared as an editorial:

"EMIGRANTS ON THE MOUNTAINS.

'It is probably not generally known to the people that there is now in the California mountains, in a most distressing situation, a party of emigrants from the United States who were prevented from crossing the mountains by an early, heavy fall of snow. The party consists of about sixty persons—men, women and children. They were almost entirely out of provisions when they reached the foot of the mountains, and but for the timely succor afforded them by Capt. J. A. Sutter, one of the most humane and liberal men in California, they must have all perished in a few days. Capt. Sutter, as soon as he ascertained their situation, sent five mules loaded with provisions to them. A second party was dispatched with provisions for them, but they found the mountain impassable in consequence of the snow. We hope that our citizens will do something for the relief of these unfortunate people."

From the same source, under date of February 6th, 1847, is taken the following:

"PUBLIC MEETING.

"It will be recollected that in a previous number of our paper we called the attention of our citizens to the situatiôn of a company of unfortunate emigrants now in the California mountains. For the purpose of making their situation more fully known to the people, and of adopting measures for their relief, a public meeting was called by the Honorable Washington A. Bartlett, Alcalde of the town, on Wednesday evening last. The citizens generally attended, and in a very short time the sum of $800 was subscribed to purchase provisions, clothing, horses and mules to bring the emigrants in. Committees were appointed to call on those who could not attend the meeting, and there is no doubt but that $500 or $600 more will be raised. This speaks well for Yerba Buena."

One other extract is quoted from the Star of February 13th, 1847 :

"COMPANY LEFT.

"A company of twenty men left here on Sunday last for the California mountains, with provisions, clothing, etc., for the suffering emigrants now there. The citizens of this place subscribed about $1,500 for their relief, which was expended for such articles as the emigrants would be most likely to need. Mr. Greenwood, an old mountaineer, went with the company as pilot. If it is possible to cross the mountains, they will get to the emigrants in time to save them."

These three articles may aid the reader in better understanding what has heretofore been said about the organization of the relief parties. It will be remembered that James F. Reed and William McCutchen first procured animals and provisions from Capt. Sutter, attempted to cross the mountains, found the snow impassable, cached their provisions and returned to the valleys. Reed, as described in his letter to the Rural Press, went to San Jose, Cal., and thence to Yerba Buena. McCutchen went to Napa and Sonoma, and awakened such an interest that a subscription of over $500 was subscribed for the emigrants, besides a number of horses and mules. Lieut. W. L. Maury and M. G. Vallejo headed this subscription, and $500 was promised to Greenwood if he succeeded in raising a company and in piloting them over the mountains. In order to get men, Greenwood and McCutchen went to Yerba Buena, arriving there almost at the same time with Reed. The above notices chronicle the events which succeeded the announcement of their mission. The funds and supplies contributed were placed in charge of Lieut.

10

Woodworth. This party set out immediately, and their journey has been described. They form the second relief party, because immediately upon the arrival of the seven who survived of the "Forlorn Hope," Capt. Tucker's party had been organized at Johnson's and Sutter's, and had reached Donner Lake first.

When Foster and Eddy attempted to form a relief party, they found the same difficulty in securing volunteers which others had encountered. It was such a terrible undertaking that no man cared to risk his life in the expedition.

Captain J. B. Hull, of the United States Navy, and Commander of the Northern District of California, furnished Foster and Eddy with horses and provisions. Setting out from Johnson's ranch, they arrived at Woodworth's camp in the afternoon. During that very night two of Reed's men came to the camp, and brought news that Reed and a portion of his party were a short distance back in the mountains. When Reed and his companions were brought into camp, and it was ascertained that fourteen people had been left in the snow, without food, the third relief party was at once organized. The great danger and suffering endured by those who had composed the first and second relief parties, prevented men from volunteering. On this account greater honor is due those who determined to peril their lives to save the emigrants. Hiram Miller, although weak and exhausted with the fatigues and starvation he had just undergone in the second relief party, joined Messrs. Foster and Eddy. These three, with Wm. Thompson, John Stark, Howard Oakley and Charles Stone, set out from Woodworth's camp the next morning after Reed's arrival.

It was agreed that Stark, Oakley and Stone were to remain with the sufferers at Starved Camp, supply them with food, and conduct them to Woodworth's camp. Foster, Eddy, Thompson and Miller were to press forward to the relief of those at Donner Lake.

When Stark and his companions reached the deep, well-like cavity in which were the seven Breens, the three Graves children and Mary Donner, a very serious question arose. None of the eleven, except Mrs. Breen and John Breen, were able to walk. A storm appeared to be gathering upon the mountains, and the supply of provisions was very limited. The lonely situation, the weird, desolate surroundings, the appalling scenes at the camp, and above all the danger of being overtaken by a snow storm, filled the minds of Oakley and Stone with terror. When it was found that nine out of the eleven people must be carried over the snow, it is hardly to be wondered at that a proposition was made to leave a portion of the sufferers. It was proposed to take the three Graves children and Mary Donner. These four children would be quite a sufficient burden for the three men, considering the snow over which they must travel. The Breens, or at least such of them as could not walk, were to be abandoned. This was equivalent to leaving the father, mother and five children, because the mother would not abandon any member of her family, and John, who alone could travel, was in a semi-lifeless condition. The members of the third relief party are said to have taken a vote upon the question. This scene is described in the manuscript of Hon. James F. Breen: "Those who were in favor of returning to the settlements and leaving the Breens for a future relief party (which, under the circumstances, was equivalent to the death penalty), were to answer 'aye.' The question was put to each man by name, and as the names were called the dreadful 'aye' responded. John Stark's name was the last one called, because he had, during the discussion of the question, strongly opposed the proposition for abandonment, and it was naturally supposed that when he found himself in so hopeless a minority he would surrender. When his name was called, he made no answer until some one said to him: 'Stark, won't you vote?' Stark, during all this proceeding of calling the roll, had stood apart from his companions with bowed head and folded arms. When he was thus directly appealed to, he answered quickly and decidedly: 'No, gentlemen, I will not abandon these people. I am here on a mission of mercy, and I will not half do the work. You can all go if you want to, but I shall stay by these people while they and I live.'"

It was nobly said. If the Breens had been left at Starved Camp, even until the return of Foster, Eddy, Miller and Thompson from the lake, none would have ever reached the settlements. In continuation of the above narration, the following is taken from the manuscript of John Breen: "Stark was finally left alone. To his great bodily strength, and unexcelled courage, myself and others owe our lives. There was probably no other man in California at that time who had the intelligence, determination, and what was absolutely necessary in that emergency, the immense physical powers of John Stark. He was as strong as two ordinary men. On his broad shoulders, he carried the provisions, most of the blankets, and most of the time some of the weaker children. In regard to this, he would laughingly say that he could carry them all, if there was room on his back, because they were so light from starvation."

By every means in his power, Stark would cheer and encourage the poor sufferers. Frequently he would carry one or two ahead a little way, put them down, and return for the others. James F. Breen says: "I distinctly remember that myself and Jonathan Graves were both carried by Stark on his back the greater part of the journey." Others speak similarly.

Regarding this brave man, Dr. J. C. Leonard has contributed much valuable information, from which is selected the following:

"John Stark was born in 1817, in Wayne County, Indiana. His father, William Stark, came from Virginia, and was one of the first settlers of Kentucky, arriving there about the same time as Daniel Boone. He married a cousin of Daniel Boone, and they had a family of eight children. T. J. Stark, the oldest son, now lives at French Corral, Nevada County. John Stark, the younger brother, started from Monmouth County, Illinois, in the Spring of 1846, but taking the Fort Hall road, reached California in safety. He was a powerfully built man, weighing two hundred and twenty pounds. He was Sheriff of Napa County for six years, and in 1852 represented that county in the State Legislature. He died near Calistoga in 1875, of heart disease. His death was instantaneous, and occurred while pitching hay from a wagon. He was the father of eleven children, six of whom, with his wife, are now living." Each one of the persons who were taken from Starved Camp by this hero and his two companions, reached Sutter's Fort in safety. James F. Breen had his feet badly frozen, and afterwards burned while at the camp. No one had any hope that they could be saved, and when the party reached the Fort, a doctor was sought to amputate them. None could be found, and kind nature effected a cure which a physician would have pronounced impossible.

In concluding this chapter it is quite appropriate to quote the following, written by J. F. Breen. "No one can attach blame to those who voted to leave part of the emigrants. It was a desperate case. Their idea was to save as many as possible, and they honestly believed that by attempting to save all, all would be lost. But this consideration—and the further one that Stark was an entire stranger to every one in the camps, not bound to them by any tie of blood or kindred, nor having any hope of reward except the grand consciousness of doing a noble act—makes his conduct shine more lustrously in the eyes of every person who admires nature's true and only nobility."

Chapter XVII.

HE death of Mrs. Elizabeth Donner occurred about the
time the second relief took their departure. After the
death of her husband, Jacob Donner, she had devoted all
her energies to the welfare of her children. Solomon Hook,
Isaac and Mary Donner, had been sent out in care of the
second relief. William Hook had gone with the first party.
Only the mother and her two youngest sons remained. The mother
was quite able to have crossed the mountains with either of these
two parties, but, as Mrs. E. P. Houghton writes: "Her little boys
were too young to walk through the deep snows. She was not able
to carry them, and the relief parties were too small to meet such
emergencies. She stayed with them, hoping some way would be
provided for their rescue. Grief, hunger, and disappointed hopes,
crushed her energies, and so debilitated her, that she and Lewis
died before the required help reached them. Samuel, the youngest,
was taken by my mother (Mrs. Tamsen Donner) to our camp, where
he lived a number of days after his mother's death." It will thus
be seen, that for her children this mother sacrificed her life. Could

words be framed to express a more fitting tribute to her memory! Does not the simple story of this mother's love wreathe a chaplet of glory about her brow far holier than could be fashioned by human hands!

When the relief party of Foster and Eddy reached Donner Lake, the sole survivors of those who encamped at Alder Creek were George Donner the Captain of the Donner Party, his faithful wife Tamsen Donner, and the Spanish boy, John Baptiste. Under the snow drifts which covered the valley lay Jacob Donner, Elizabeth Donner, Lewis Donner, Samuel Donner, Samuel Shoemaker, Jos. Rhinehart, and James Smith. One more was soon to be added to the number. It was the man whose name had been given to the company; the only one who died of a lingering, painful disease. The injury of George Donner's hand had grown into a feverish, virulent ulceration, which must have partaken of the nature of erysipelas. At all events mortification had set in, and when the third relief party arrived, it had reached his shoulder. In a few hours at most, he must die.

During the tearful days which elapsed between Reed's departure and Foster's arrival, much suffering occurred at Donner Lake. Mrs. Lavina Murphy had charge of her son, Simon Murphy, her grandchild, George Foster, of the child James Eddy, and of the three little Donner girls, Frances, Georgia, and Eliza. All dwelt in the same cabin, and with them was Lewis Keseberg. Foster and Eddy found all there, save their own children. They were both dead. Keseberg has generally been accused of the murder of little George Foster. Except Mrs. Murphy, the oldest of those who were with Keseberg was only nine years of age. All that the children know is that Keseberg took the child to bed with him one night, and that it was dead next morning. One of the little ones who survived—one whose memory has proven exceedingly truthful upon all points wherein her evidence could be possibly substantiated—one who is now, Mrs. Georgia A. Babcock—gives the mildest version of this sad affair which has ever appeared in print. She denies the story, so often reiterated, that Keseberg took the child to bed with him and

ate it up before morning ; but writes the following : " In the morning the child was dead.   Mrs. Murphy took it, sat down near the
bed where my sister and myself were lying, laid the little one on
her lap, and made remarks to other persons, accusing Keseberg of
killing it.   After awhile he came, took it from her, and hung it up
in sight, inside the cabin, on the wall."

Foster, Eddy, Thompson and Miller remained but a little while at
the mountain camp.   During this time Mr. Foster had no opportunity to talk with Mrs. Murphy save in Keseberg's presence.   Afterwards, when the children told him of the suspicions expressed in
their presence by Mrs. Murphy, Foster deeply regretted that he had
not sought a private interview with her, for the purpose of learning
the reasons for her belief.

In the morning the relief party was to start back to the settlements.   Eddy was to carry Georgia Donner ; Thompson, Frances
Donner ;   Miller, Eliza Donner, and Foster was to carry Simon
Murphy.   John Baptiste and the man Clark were to accompany
the party.   This left Mr. and Mrs. Donner at Alder Creek, and
Keseberg and Mrs. Murphy at the cabins.   Mrs. Murphy had
cared for her children and her grand-children, and ministered to the
wants of those around her, until she was sick, exhausted, and utterly
helpless.   She could not walk.   She could scarcely rise from her
bed.   With all the tenderness of a son, Mr. Foster gave her such
provisions as he could leave, procured her wood, and did whatever
he was able to do to render her comfortable.   He also promised to
return speedily, and with such assistance that he could carry her
over the summits to her children.

The very afternoon that the third relief party reached the cabins,
Simon Murphy discovered a woman wandering about in the snow
as if lost.   It proved to be Mrs. Tamsen Donner.   She had wearily
traveled over the deep snows from Alder Creek, to see if there were
any tidings from her children.   To her surprise she found they had
not been taken over the mountains.   Oh ! the joy and the pain of
the meeting of those little ones and their mother.   As they wound
their arms about her neck, kissed her lips, laughed in her eyes, and

twined their fingers in her hair, what a struggle must have been taking place in her soul. As the pleading, upturned faces of her babies begged her not to leave them, her very heart-strings must have been rent with agony. Well may the voice quiver or the hand tremble, that attempts to portray the anguish of this mother during that farewell interview. From the very first moment, her resolution to return to her husband remained unshaken. The members of the relief party entreated her to go with her children and save her own life. They urged that there could only be a few hours of life left in George Donner. This was so true that she once ventured the request that they remain until she could return to Alder Creek, and see if he were yet alive. The gathering storm-clouds which had hovered over the summit for days, compelled them to refuse this request. An hour's delay might be fatal to all.

George Donner knew that he was dying, and had frequently urged his wife to leave him, cross the mountains, and take care of her children. As she held her darlings in her arms, it required no prophetic vision to disclose pictures of sadness, of lonely childhood, of longing girlhood, of pillows wet with tears, if these three little waifs were left to wander friendless in California. She never expressed a belief that she would see that land of promise beyond the Sierras. Often had her calm, earnest voice told them of the future which awaited them, and so far as possible had she prepared them to meet that future without the counsel or sympathy of father or mother.

The night-shadows, creeping through the shivering pines, warned her of the long, dreary way over which her tired feet must pass ere she reached her dying husband's side. She is said to have appeared strangely composed. The struggle was silent. The poor bleeding heart brought not a single moan to the lips. It was a choice between life, hope and her clinging babes, or a lonely vigil by a dying husband, and an unknown, shroudless death in the wintry mountains. Her husband was sixty-three; he was well stricken in years, and his life was fast ebbing away. If she returned through the frosty night-winds, over the crisp, freezing snow, she would travel fourteen miles that day. The strong, healthy men composing the relief parties

frequently could travel but five or six miles in a day. If she made
the journey, and found her husband was dead, she could have no
hope of returning on the morrow. She had suffered too long from
hunger and privation to hope to be able to return and overtake the
relief party. It was certain life or certain death. On the side of
the former was maternal love ; on the side of the latter, wifely devotion. The whole wide range of history cannot produce a parallel
example of adherence to duty, and to the dictates of conjugal fidelity.
With quick convulsive pressure of her little ones to her heart ; with
a hasty, soul-throbbing kiss upon the lips of each ; with a prayer that
was stifled with a sob of agony, Tamsen Donner hurried away to her
husband. Through the gathering darkness, past the shadowy senti-
nels of the forest, they watched with tearful eyes her retreating form.
As if she dared not trust another sight of the little faces—as if to
escape the pitiful wail of her darlings—she ran straight forward until
out of sight and hearing. She never once looked back.

There are mental struggles which so absorb the being and soul,
that physical terrors or tortures are unnoticed. Tamsen Donner's
mind was passing through such an ordeal. The fires of Moloch, the
dreadful suttee, were sacrifices which long religious education sanc-
tioned, and in which the devotees perished amidst the plaudits of
admiring multitudes. This woman had chosen a death of solitude,
of hunger, of bitter cold, of pain-racked exhaustion, and was actuated
by only the pure principles of wifely love. Already the death-damp
was gathering on George Donner's brow. At the utmost, she could
hope to do no more than smooth the dying pillow, tenderly clasp the
fast-chilling hand, press farewell kisses upon the whitening lips, and
finally close the dear tired eyes. For this, only this, she was yielding
life, the world and her darling babes. Fitted by culture and refinement to be an ornament to society, qualified by education to rear her
daughters to lives of honor and usefulness, how it must have wrung
her heart to allow her little ones to go unprotected into a wilderness
of strangers. But she could not leave her husband to die alone.
Rather solitude, better death, than desert the father of her children.
O Land of the Sunset ! let the memory of this wife's devotion be

ever enshrined in the hearts of your faithful daughters! In tablets thus pure engrave the name of Tamsen Donner.

When the June sunshine gladdened the Sacramento Valley, three sweet little barefooted girls walked here and there among the houses and tents of Sutter's Fort. They were scantily clothed, and one carried a thin blanket. At night they said their prayers, lay down in whatever tent they happened to be, and folding the blanket about them fell asleep in each other's arms. When they were hungry they asked food of whomsoever they met. If any one inquired who they were, they answered as their mother had taught them: "We are the children of Mr. and Mrs. George Donner." But they added something they had learned since. It was, "and our parents are dead."

CHAPTER XVIII.

KESEBERG is one of the leading characters in the Donner
Party. Usually, his part in the tragedy has been considered
the entire story. Comparatively few people have understood that any except this one man ate human flesh, or was
a witness of any scene of horror. He has been loathed,
execrated, abhorred as a cannibal, a murderer and a heartless fiend. In the various published sketches which have from time
to time been given to the world, Lewis Keseberg has been charged
with no less than six murders. His cannibalism has been denounced
as arising from choice, as growing out of a depraved and perverted
appetite, instead of being the result of necessity. On the 4th of April,
1879, this strange man granted an interview to the author, and in
this and succeeding interviews he reluctantly made a statement which
was reduced to writing. "What is the use," he would urge, "of my
making a statement? People incline to believe the most horrible
reports concerning a man, and they will not credit what I say in my
own defense. My conscience is clear. I am an old man, and am
calmly awaiting my death. God is my judge, and it long ago ceased
to trouble me that people shunned and slandered me."

Keseberg is six feet in height, is well proportioned, and weighs from one hundred and seventy-five to one hundred and eighty pounds. He is active, vigorous, and of an erect, manly carriage, despite his years and his many afflictions. He has clear blue eyes, regular features, light hair and beard, a distinct, rapid mode of enunciation, a loud voice, and a somewhat excited manner of speech. In conversing he looks one squarely and steadily in the eye, and appears like an honest, intelligent German. He speaks and writes German, French, Spanish and English, and his selection of words proves him a scholar. His face generally wears a determined, almost fierce expression, but one is impressed with the thought that this appearance is caused by his habitually standing on the defensive as against his fellow men. Since he has never before had an opportunity of speaking in his own defense, it is perhaps fitting that his statement should be given in his own language:

"My name is Lewis Keseberg. I was born in the City of Berleburg, Province of Westphalia, in the Kingdom of Prussia, on the 22d of May, 1814. I am therefore almost sixty-three years of age. I was married June 22d, 1842, came to the United States May 22d, 1844, and emigrated to California in 1846 with the Donner Party. I never have made a statement concerning my connection with that Party to any one connected with the press. It is with the utmost horror that I revert to the scenes of suffering and unutterable misery endured during that journey. I have always endeavored to put away from me all thoughts or recollections of those terrible events. Time is the best physician, and would, I trusted, heal the wounds' produced by those days of torture; yet my mind to-day recoils with undiminished horror, as I endeavor to speak of this dreadful subject. Heretofore I have never attempted to refute the villainous slanders which have been circulated and published about me. I feel it my duty to make this statement, however, because I am convinced of your willingness to do justice to all who were concerned in that dreadful affair, and heretofore I have been treated with gross injustice.

"If I believe in God Almighty having anything to do with the affairs of men, I believe that the misfortune which overtook the Donner Party, and the terrible part I was compelled to take in the great tragedy, were predestined. On the Hastings Cut-off we were twenty-eight days in going twenty-one miles. Difficulty and disaster hovered about us from the time we entered upon this cut-off.

"One day while we were traveling on Goose Creek, we saw so many wild geese that I took my shotgun and went hunting. Ordinarily I am not superstitious, but on this morning I felt an overwhelming sense of impending calamity. I mentioned my premonitions to Mrs. Murphy before starting on the hunt. Becoming excited with the sport, and eagerly watching the game, I stepped down a steep bank. Some willows had been burned off, and the short, sharp stubs were sticking up just where I stepped. I had on buckskin moccasins, and one of these stubs ran into the ball of my foot between the bones of the toes. From this time until we arrived at Donner Lake I was unable to walk, or even to put my foot to the ground. The foot became greatly swollen and inflamed, and was exceedingly painful. One day at Donner Lake, one of my companions, at my earnest request, lanced my foot on the top. It discharged freely, and some days afterwards, in washing it, I found a hard substance protruding from the wound, and obtaining a pair of forceps, succeeded in extracting a piece of the willow stub one and a half inches in length. It had literally worked up through my foot. I mention this particularly, because I have been frequently accused of remaining at the Donner cabins for selfish or sinister motives, when in fact I was utterly unable to join the relief parties."

It is proper to mention, in corroboration of Keseberg's statement regarding his lameness, that several of the survivors remembered, and had related the circumstance prior to the interview. It is a well authenticated fact that he was very lame, and could not walk, yet as a specimen of the abuse which has been heaped upon the man, a quotation is introduced from Thornton's "Oregon and California." In speaking of the departure of Foster and Eddy, Thornton says: "There were in camp Mrs. Murphy, Mr. and Mrs. George Donner, and Keseberg—the latter, it was believed, having far more strength to travel than others who had arrived in the settlements. But he would not travel, for the reason, as was suspected, that he wished to remain behind for the purpose of obtaining the property and money of the dead." Keseberg's statement continues :

"When we reached the lake we lost our road, and owing to the depth of the snow on the mountains, were compelled to abandon our wagons, and pack our goods upon oxen. The cattle, unused to such burdens, caused great delay by 'bucking' and wallowing in the snow. There was also much confusion as to what articles should be taken and what abandoned. One wanted a box of tobacco carried along; another, a bale of calico, and some one thing and some another. But for this delay we would have passed the summit and pressed forward to California. Owing to my lameness, I was placed on horseback, and my foot was tied up to the saddle in a sort of sling. Near evening we were close to the top of the dividing ridge. It was cold and chilly, and everybody was tired with the severe exertions of the day. Some of the emigrants sat down to rest, and declared they could go no further. I begged them for God's sake to get over the ridge before halting. Some one, however, set fire to a pitchy pine tree, and the flames soon ascended to its topmost branches. The women and children gathered about this fire to warm themselves. Meantime the oxen were rubbing off their packs against the trees. The weather looked very threatening, and I exhorted them to go on until the summit was reached. I foresaw the danger plainly and unmistakably. Only the strongest men, however, could go ahead and break the road, and it would have taken a determined man to induce the party to leave the fire. Had I been well, and been able to push ahead over the ridge, some, if not all, would have followed. As it was, all laid down on the snow, and from exhaustion were soon asleep. In the night, I felt something impeding my breath. A heavy weight seemed to be resting upon me. Springing up to a sitting posture, I found myself covered with freshly-fallen snow. The camp, the cattle, my companions, had all disappeared. All I could see was snow everywhere. I shouted at the top of my voice. Suddenly, here and there, all about me,

heads popped up through the snow. The scene was not unlike what
one might imagine at the resurrection, when people rise up out of
the earth.   The terror amounted to a panic.   The mules were lost,
the cattle strayed away, and our further progress rendered impossible.
The rest you probably know.   We returned to the lake, and prepared as best we could for the Winter.   I was unable to build a
cabin, because of my lameness, and so erected a sort of brush shed
against one side of Breen's cabin.

"When Reed's relief party left the cabins, Mr. Reed left me a half
teacupful of flour, and about half a pound of jerked beef.   It was all
he could give.   Mrs. Murphy, who was left with me, because too
weak and emaciated to walk, had no larger portion.   Reed had
no animosity against me.   He found me too weak to move.   He
washed me, combed my hair, and treated me kindly.   Indeed, he
had no cause to do otherwise.   When Reed came with the relief
party to the lake, he found his children in my cabin.   Some of my
portion of the flour brought by Stanton from Sutter's Fort I gave to
Reed's children, and thus saved their lives.   When he left me, he
promised to return in two weeks and carry me over the mountains.
When this party left I was not able to stand, much less to walk.

"A heavy storm came on in a few days after the last relief party
left.   Mrs. George Donner had remained with her sick husband in
their camp, six or seven miles away.   Mrs. Murphy lived about a
week after we were left alone.   When my provisions gave out I
remained four days before I could taste human flesh.   There was
no other resort—it was that or death.   My wife and child had gone
on with the first relief party.   I knew not whether they were living
or dead.   They were penniless and friendless in a strange land.   For
their sakes I must live if not for my own.   Mrs. Murphy was too
weak to revive.   The flesh of starved beings contains little nutriment.
It is like feeding straw to horses.   I cannot describe the unutterable
repugnance with which I tasted the first mouthful of flesh.   There
is an instinct in our nature that revolts at the thought of touching,
much less eating, a corpse.   It makes my blood curdle to think of
it !   It has been told that I boasted of my shame—said that I

enjoyed this horrid food, and that I remarked that human flesh was more palatable than California beef. This is a falsehood. It is a horrible, revolting falsehood. This food was never otherwise than loathsome, insipid and disgusting. For nearly two months I was alone in that dismal cabin. No one knows what occurred but myself—no living being ever before was told of the occurrences. Life was a burden. The horrors of one day succeeded those of the preceding. Five of my companions had died in my cabin, and their stark and ghastly bodies lay there day and night, seemingly gazing at me with their glazed and staring eyes. I was too weak to move them had I tried. The relief parties had not removed them. These parties had been too hurried, too horror-stricken at the sight, too fearful lest an hour's delay might cause them to share the same fate. I endured a thousand deaths. To have one's suffering prolonged inch by inch, to be deserted, forsaken, hopeless ; to see that loathsome food ever before my eyes, was almost too much for human endurance. I am conversant with four different languages. I speak and write them with equal fluency, yet in all four I do not find words enough to express the horror I experienced during those two months, or what I still feel when memory reverts to the scene. Suicide would have been a relief, a happiness, a godsend ! Many a time I had the muzzle of my pistol in my mouth and my finger on the trigger, but the faces of my helpless, dependent wife and child would rise up before me, and my hand would fall powerless. I was not the cause of my misfortunes, and God Almighty had provided only this one horrible way for me to subsist."

Did you boil the flesh ?

"Yes ! But to go into details—to relate the minutiæ—is too agonizing ! I cannot do it ! Imagination can supply these. The necessary mutilation of the bodies of those who had been my friends, rendered the ghastliness of my situation more frightful. When I could crawl about and my lame foot was partially recovered, I was chopping some wood one day and the ax glanced and cut off my

11

heel. The piece of flesh grew back in time, but not in its former position, and my foot is maimed to this day.

"A man before he judges me, should be placed in a similar situation ; but if he were, it is a thousand to one he would perish. A constitution of steel alone could endure the deprivation and misery. At this time I was living in the log cabin with the fireplace. One night I was awakened by a scratching sound over my head. I started up in terror, and listened intently for the noise to be repeated. It came again. It was the wolves trying to get into the cabin to eat me and the dead bodies.

"At midnight, one cold, bitter night, Mrs. George Donner came to my door. It was about two weeks after Reed had gone, and my loneliness was beginning to be unendurable. I was most happy to hear the sound of a human voice. Her coming was like that of an angel from Heaven. But she had not come to bear me company. Her husband had died in her arms. She had remained by his side until death came, and then had laid him out and hurried away. He died at nightfall, and she had traveled over the snow alone to my cabin. She was going, alone, across the mountains. She was going to start without food or guide. She kept saying, ' My children ! I must see my children !' She feared she would not survive, and told me she had some money in her tent. It was too heavy for her to carry. She said, ' Mr. Keseberg, I confide this to your care.' She made me promise sacredly that I would get the money and take it to her children in case she perished and I survived. She declared she would start over the mountains in the morning. She said, ' I am bound to go to my children.' She seemed very cold, and her clothes were like ice. I think she had got in the creek in coming. She said she was very hungry, but refused the only food I could offer. She had never eaten the loathsome flesh. She finally laid down, and I spread a feather bed and some blankets over her. In the morning she was dead. I think the hunger, the mental suffering, and the icy chill of the preceding night, caused her death. I have often been accused of taking her life. Before my God, I swear this is untrue ! Do you think a man would be such a miscreant, such a damnable fiend, such a caricature on humanity, as to kill this lone woman? There were plenty of corpses lying around. He would only add one more corpse to the many!

"Oh! the days and weeks of horror which I passed in that camp! I had no hope of help or of being rescued, until I saw the green grass coming up by the spring on the hillside, and the wild geese coming to nibble it. The birds were coming back to their breeding grounds, and I felt that I could kill them for food. I had plenty of guns and ammunition in camp. I also had plenty of tobacco and a good meerschaum pipe, and almost the only solace I enjoyed was smoking. In my weak condition it took me two or three hours every day to get sufficient wood to keep my fire going.

"Some time after Mrs. Donner's death, I thought I had gained sufficient strength to redeem the pledge I had made her before her death. I started to go to the camps at Alder Creek to get the money. I had a very difficult journey. The wagons of the Donners were loaded with tobacco, powder, caps, shoes, school-books, and dry-goods. This stock was very valuable, and had it reached California, would have been a fortune to the Donners. I searched carefully among the bales and bundles of goods, and found $531. Part of this sum was silver, part gold. The silver I buried at the foot of a pine tree, a little way from the camp. One of the lower branches of another tree reached down close to the ground, and appeared to point to the spot. I put the gold in my pocket, and started to return to my cabin. I had spent one night at the Donner tents. On my return I became lost. When it was nearly dark, in crossing a little flat, the snow suddenly gave way under my feet, and I sank down almost to my armpits. By means of the crust on top of the snow, I kept myself suspended by throwing out my arms. A stream of water flowed underneath the place over which I had been walking, and the snow had melted on the underside until it was not strong enough to support my weight. I could not touch bottom with my feet, and so could form no idea of the depth of the stream. By long and careful exertion, I managed to draw myself backward and up on the snow. I then went around on the hillside, and continued my journey. At last, just at dark, completely exhausted and almost dead, I came in sight of the Graves cabin. I shall never forget my joy at sight of that log cabin. I felt that I was no longer lost, and would at least have shelter. Some time after dark I reached my own cabin. My clothes were wet by getting in the creek, and the night was so cold that my garments were frozen into sheets of ice. I was so weary, and chilled, and numbed that I did not build up a fire, or attempt to get anything to eat, but rolled myself up in the bed-clothes and tried to get warm. Nearly all night I lay there shivering with cold, and when I finally slept, I slept very soundly. I did not wake up until quite late the next morning. To my utter astonishment my camp was in the most inexplicable confusion. My trunks were broken open, and their contents were scattered everywhere. Everything about the cabin was torn up and thrown about the floor. My wife's jewelry, my cloak, my pistol and ammunition were missing. I supposed Indians had robbed my camp during my absence. Suddenly I was startled by the sound of human voices. I hurried up to the surface of the snow, and saw white men coming towards the cabin. I was overwhelmed with joy and gratitude at the prospect of my deliverance. I had suffered so much, and for so long a time, that I could scarcely believe my senses. Imagine my astonishment upon their arrival to be greeted, not with a 'good morning' or a kind word, but with the gruff, insolent demand, 'Where is Donner's money?'

"I told them they ought to give me something to eat, and that I would talk with them afterwards, but no, they insisted that I should tell them about Donner's money. I asked them who they were, and where they came from, but they replied by threatening to kill me if I did not give up the money. They threatened to hang or shoot me, and at last I told them I had promised Mrs. Donner that I would carry her money to her children, and I proposed to do so unless shown some authority by which they had a better claim. This so exasperated them that they acted as though they were going to kill me. I offered to let them bind me as a prisoner, and take me before the Alcalde at Sutter's Fort, and I promised that I would then tell all

I knew about the money. They would listen to nothing, however, and finally, to save my life, I told them where they would find the silver buried, and gave them the gold. After I had done this, they showed me a document from Alcalde Sinclair by which they were to receive a certain proportion of all moneys and property which they rescued."

The men spoken of by Keseberg, were the fourth relief party. Their names were Captain Fallon, William M. Foster, John Rhodes, J. Foster, R. P. Tucker, E. Coffeemire, and —— Keyser. William M. Foster had recrossed the mountains the second time, hoping to rescue his wife's mother, Mrs. Murphy. Alas! he found only her mutilated remains.

CHAPTER XIX.

ECEMBER 16th, 1846, the fifteen composing the "Forlorn
Hope," left Donner Lake. January 17th, 1847, they reached
Johnson's ranch, and February 5th Capt. Tucker's party
started to the assistance of the emigrants. This first relief
arrived February 19th at the cabins; the second relief, or
Reed's party, arrived March 1st; the third, or Foster's, about
the middle of March, and the fourth, or Fallon's, on the 17th of
April. Upon the arrival of Capt. Fallon's company, the sight presented at the cabins beggars all description. Capt. R. P. Tucker,
now of Goleta, Santa Barbara County, Cal., endeavors, in his cor-
respondence, to give a slight idea of the scene. Human bodies,
terribly mutilated, legs, arms, skulls and portions of remains, were
scattered in every direction and strewn about the camp. Mr. Foster
found Mrs. Murphy's body with one of her limbs sawed off, the saw
still lying by her remains. It was such scenes as these which gave
this party their first abhorrence for Keseberg. The man was nowhere
to be seen, but a fresh track was discovered in the snow leading
away from the cabins toward the Donner tents. The party pressed

forward to Alder Creek.   Captain Tucker writes : " The dead bodies
lay mouldering around, being all that was left to tell the tale of sor-
row.   On my first trip we had cut down a large pine tree and laid
the goods of the Donners on this tree to dry in the sun.   These
goods lay there yet, with the exception of those which Reed's party
had taken away."

George Donner was supposed to be wealthy.   His wealth consisted
not merely of goods, as many claim, but of a large amount of coin.
Hiram Miller, of the relief parties, is authority for the statement that
Mr. Donner owned a quarter section of land within the present city
limits of Chicago.   This land was sold for ten thousand dollars
shortly before Mr. Donner started for California.   Mr. Allen Francis,
who has been mentioned as the very best authority concerning this
family, camped with them on the evening of their first night's journey
out of Springfield, Illinois, saw Mr. Donner's money, and thinks
there was ten thousand dollars.   Mrs. F. E. Bond, of Elk Grove,
Sacramento County, California, does not remember the exact amount,
but knows that Mr. Donner started with a great deal of gold, because
she helped to make the belts in which it was to be carried in crossing
the plains.   The relief parties always understood there was at Donner's camp a large sum of money, estimated at from six to fourteen
thousand dollars.   It is not disputed that Halloran left about fifteen
hundred dollars to this family.   Yet Capt. Fallon's party could find
no money.   It was clear to their minds that some one had robbed
the Donner tents.

Remaining over night, thoroughly searching in every place where
they supposed money could be concealed, this party returned to
Donner Lake.   On their way they found the same mysterious track,
also returning to the cabins.   They probably discovered Keseberg
in about the manner described.   It is plain to be seen that they
regarded him as the murderer of Mrs. Donner.   In forcing him to
tell what he had done with the money, they, too, claim to have
choked him, to have put a rope around his neck, and to have threatened to hang him.   On the other hand, if Keseberg's statement be
accepted as truth, it is easy to understand why he refused to surren-

der the money to men who treated him from the outset as a murderer
and a robber.

Let the God to whom Lewis Keseberg appeals, be his judge.   It
is not the part of this book to condemn or acquit him.   Most of the
fourth relief party have already gone before the bar at which Keseberg asks to be tried.   Capt. Tucker is about the only available
witness, and his testimony is far more lenient than the rumors and
falsehoods usually published.

If Keseberg be guilty of any or of all crimes, it will presently be
seen that the most revengeful being on earth could not ask that
another drop be added to his cup of bitterness.   His statement continues :

"These men treated me with the greatest unkindness.   Mr. Tucker
was the only one who took my part or befriended me.   When they
started over the mountains, each man carried two bales of goods.
They had silks, calicos and delaines from the Donners, and other
articles of great value.   Each man would carry one bundle a little
way, lay it down and come back and get the other bundle.   In this
way they passed over the snow three times.   I could not keep up
with them because I was so weak, but managed to come up to their
camp every night.   One day I was dragging myself slowly along
behind the party, when I came to a place which had evidently been
used as a camping ground by some of the previous parties.   Feeling
very tired, I thought it would be a good place to make some coffee.
Kindling a fire, I filled my coffee-pot with fresh snow and sat waiting
for it to melt and get hot.   Happening to cast my eyes carelessly
around, I discovered a little piece of calico protruding from the snow.
Half thoughtlessly, half out of idle curiosity, I caught hold of the
cloth, and finding it did not come readily, I gave it a strong pull.   I
had in my hands the body of my dead child Ada !   She had been
buried in the snow, which melting down had disclosed a portion of
her clothing.   I thought I should go frantic !   It was the first inti-
mation I had of her death, and it came with such a shock !

"Just as we were getting out of the snow, I happened to be
sitting in camp, alone, one afternoon.   The men were hunting, or

attending to their goods. I was congratulating myself upon my escape from the mountains, when I was startled by a snuffling, growling noise, and looking up, I saw a large grizzly bear only a few feet away. I knew I was too weak to attempt to escape, and so remained where I sat, expecting every moment he would devour me. Suddenly there was the report of a gun, and the bear fell dead. Mr. Foster had discovered the animal, and slipping up close to camp, had killed it."

When the party arrived at Sutter's Fort, they took no pains to conceal their feelings toward Keseberg. Some of the men openly accused him of Mrs. Donner's murder. Keseberg, at the suggestion of Captain Sutter, brought action against Captain Fallon, Ned Coffeemire and the others, for slander. The case was tried before Alcalde Sinclair, and the jury gave Keseberg a verdict of one dollar damages. The old Alcalde records are not in existence, but some of the survivors remember the circumstance, and Mrs. Samuel Kyburz, now of Clarksville, El Dorado County, was a witness at the trial. If Keseberg was able to vindicate himself in an action for slander against the evidence of all the party, it is clear that such evidence was not adduced as has frequently appeared in books. For instance, in Capt. Fallon's report of this trip he alleges that "in the cabin with Keseberg were found two kettles of human blood, in all supposed to be over one gallon." Had this been proven, no jury would have found for Keseberg. Fresh blood could not have been obtained from starved bodies, and had the blood been found, Keseberg would have been adjudged a murderer.

Speaking upon this point, Keseberg denies the assertion that any blood was discovered, calls attention to the length of time Mrs. Donner had been dead, to the readiness with which blood coagulates, and adds that not a witness testified to such a circumstance at the trial. Why should Keseberg murder Mrs. Donner? If he wanted her money, it was only necessary to allow her to go out into the mountains alone, without provisions, without any one to point out the way, and perish in the trackless snows. She could not carry any considerable portion of her money with her, and he had only to go back to Alder

Creek and secure the treasure. He bears witness that she never tasted human flesh; that she would not partake of the food he offered; how reasonable, then, the story of her death. The fourth relief party expected to find a vast sum of money. One half was to be given them for their trouble. They regarded the man Keseberg as the murderer of George Foster, because of the reports given by the little children brought out by the third relief. The father of this child was with both the third and fourth reliefs. Arriving at the cabins they were amazed and horrified at the dreadful sights. Hastening to the tents, they found no money. Their idea that Keseberg was a thief was confirmed by his disgorging the money when threatened with death. There was much reason for the hatred of the man who crossed the mountains with them, and this was intensified by their being brought before Alcalde Sinclair and proven slanderers. Out of this hatred has grown reports which time has magnified into the hideous falsehoods which greet the ear from all directions. Keseberg may be responsible for the death of Hardcoop, but urges in his defense that all were walking, even to the women and the children. He says Hardcoop was not missed until evening, and that it was supposed the old man would catch up with the train during the night. The terrible dangers surrounding the company, the extreme lateness of the season, the weakness of the oxen, and the constant fear of lurking hostile Indians, prevented him or any one else from going back. Keseberg may be responsible for the death of Wolfinger, of George Foster, of James Eddy, of Mrs. Murphy, and of Mrs. Tamsen Donner, but the most careful searcher for evidence cannot find the slightest trace of proofs. In his own mournful language, he comes near the truth when he says:

"I have been born under an evil star! Fate, misfortune, bad luck, compelled me to remain at Donner Lake. If God would decree that I should again pass through such an ordeal, I could not do otherwise than I did. My conscience is free from reproach. Yet that camp has been the one burden of my life. Wherever I have gone, people have cried, 'Stone him! stone him!' Even the little children in the streets have mocked me and thrown stones at me as

I passed. Only a man conscious of his innocence, and clear in the sight of God, would not have succumbed to the terrible things which have been said of me—would not have committed suicide ! Mortification, disgrace, disaster, and unheard-of misfortune, have followed and overwhelmed me. I often think that the Almighty has singled me out, among all the men on the face of the earth, in order to see how much hardship, suffering, and misery, a human being can bear !

"Soon after my arrival at the Fort, I took charge of the schooner Sacramento, and conveyed wheat from Sacramento to San Francisco, in payment for Capt. Sutter's purchase of the Russian possessions. I worked seven months for Sutter, but, although he was kind to me, I did not get my money. I then went to Sonoma, and worked about the same length of time for Gen. Vallejo. I had a good position, and good prospects, but left for the gold mines. Soon afterward I was taken sick, and for eight months was an invalid. I then went to Sutter's Fort and started a boarding-house. I made money rapidly. After a time, I built a house, south of the Fort, which cost ten thousand dollars. In 1851, I purchased the Lady Adams Hotel, in Sacramento. It was a valuable property, and I finally sold it at auction for a large sum of money. This money was to be paid next day. The deeds had already passed. That night the terrible fire of 1852 occurred, and not only swept away the hotel, but ruined the purchaser so that I could not collect one cent. I went back to Sutter's Fort and started the Phœnix Brewery. I succeeded, and acquired considerable property. I finally sold out for fifty thousand dollars. I had concluded to take this money, go back to Germany, and live quietly the rest of my days. The purchaser went to San Francisco to draw the money. The sale was effected eight days before the great flood of 1861–2. The flood came, and I lost everything."

Thus, throughout his entire career, have business reverses followed Lewis Keseberg. Several times he has been wealthy and honorably situated. At one time he was a partner of Sam. Brannan, in a mammoth distillery at Calistoga ; and Mr. Brannan is one among many who speak in highest terms of his honesty, integrity, and business

capacity.   On the 30th of January, 1877, Phillipine Keseberg, his
faithful wife, died.   This was the severest loss of all, as will presently be seen.

Eleven children were born to them, and four are now living.   One
of these, Lillie, now lives in Sacramento, with her husband.   Another,
Paulina, a widow, resides in San Rafael.   Bertha and Augusta
live with the father at Brighton, Sacramento County.   Both these
children are hopelessly idiotic.   Bertha is twenty-six years of age,
and has never uttered an intelligible word.   Augusta is fifteen years
old, weighs two hundred and five pounds, and possesses only slight
traces of intelligence.   Teething spasms occurring when they were
about two years old, is the cause of their idiocy.   Both are subject
to frequent and violent spasms or epileptic fits.   They need constant
care and attention.   Should Bertha's hand fall in the fire, she has
not sufficient intelligence to withdraw it from the flames.   Both are
helpless as children.   The State provides for insane, but not for
idiots.   Keseberg says a bill setting aside a ward in the State
Asylum for his two children, passed the Legislature, but received a
pocket veto by the Governor.   Sacramento County gives them eighteen dollars a month.   Their helplessness and violence renders it
impossible to keep any nurse in charge of them longer than a
few days.   Keseberg is very poor.   He has employment for perhaps
three months during the year.   While his wife lived, she took care
of these children; but now he has to personally watch over them
and provide for their necessities.   While at work, he is compelled to
keep them locked in a room in the same building.   They scream so
loudly while going into the spasms that he cannot dwell near other
people.   He therefore lives isolated, in a plain little house back of
his brewery.   Here he lives, the saddest, loneliest, most pitiable
creature on the face of the earth.   He traces all his misfortunes to
that cabin on Donner Lake, and it is little wonder that he says:
" I beg of you, insert in your book a fervent prayer to Almighty God
that He will forever prevent the recurrence of a similar scene of
horror."

CHAPTER XX.

WITH the arrival of the emigrants at places of safety, this history properly closes. The members of the Donner Party were actively and intimately associated with all the early pioneer history of the State. The life of almost every one would furnish foundation for a most interesting biographical sketch. Ninety names were mentioned in the first chapter. Of these forty-two perished. Mrs. Sarah Keyes, Halloran, John Snyder, Hardcoop, Wolfinger and William M. Pike did not live to reach the mountain camps. The first victim of starvation, Baylis Williams, died in the Graves cabin. About this time Jacob Donner, Samuel Shoemaker, Joseph Rhinehart and James Smith perished at Alder Creek. The five deaths last mentioned occurred within one week, about the middle of December. During the journey of the "Forlorn Hope," the fifteen were reduced to seven by the deaths of C. T. Stanton, F. W. Graves, Antoine, Patrick Dolan, Lemuel Murphy, Jay Fosdick, Lewis and Salvador. Meantime, enrolled on the death-list at Donner Lake, were the names of Charles Burger, Lewis Keseberg, Jr., John Landrum Murphy, Margaret Eddy, Harriet McCutchen, Augustus Spitzer, Mrs. Eleanor Eddy, Milton Elliott and Catherine Pike.

During the journey of the first relief party, Ada Keseberg, John Denton and William Hook perished, and with the second relief party died Mrs. Elizabeth Graves, Isaac Donner and F. W. Graves, Jr. About this time, at the tents, died Lewis Donner, Mrs. Elizabeth Donner and Samuel Donner, George Foster and James Eddy. No deaths occurred in the party of the third relief, and no names are to be added to the fatal list save Mrs. Lavina Murphy, George Donner and Mrs. Tamsen Donner.

Out of the Donner Party, forty-eight survived. Walter Herron reached California with James F. Reed, and did not return. Of the "Forlorn Hope," Mary A. Graves, Mrs. Sarah Fosdick, Mrs. Amanda M. McCutchen, Mrs. Harriet F. Pike, Mrs. S. A. C. Foster, William M. Foster and W. H. Eddy lived. The two last mentioned returned and again braved the dangers which encompassed the emigrants. The first relief party rescued Mrs. Margaret W. Reed, Virginia E. Reed and James F. Reed, Jr., Elitha C. Donner, Leanna C. Donner, George Donner, Jr., Wm. G. Murphy, Mary M. Murphy, Naomi L. Pike, W. C. Graves, Eleanor Graves, Lovina Graves, Mrs. Phillipine Keseberg, Edward J. Breen, Simon P. Breen, Eliza Williams, Noah James and Mrs. Wolfinger.

The second relief succeeded in reaching the settlements with only Solomon Hook, Patty Reed and Thomas K. Reed. With this party were its Captain, James F. Reed, and William McCutchen. Those who were brought to Starved Camp by the second relief, and saved by a portion of the third relief, were Patrick Breen, Mrs. Margaret Breen, John Breen, Patrick Breen, Jr., James F. Breen, Peter Breen, Isabella M. Breen, Nancy Graves, Jonathan Graves, Elizabeth Graves and Mary M. Donner. The remainder of the third relief rescued Simon P. Murphy, Frances E. Donner, Georgia A. Donner, Eliza P. Donner and John Baptiste. W. H. Eddy remained in the valleys after making this journey. Wm. M. Foster traversed the snow-belt no less than five times. Once with the "Forlorn Hope," twice with the third relief, and twice with the fourth. The fourth relief rescued Lewis Keseberg.

General Kearney visited the cabins at Donner Lake on the 22d of June, 1847. Edwin Bryant, the author of "What I saw in California," was with General Kearney, and says: "A halt was ordered for the purpose of collecting and interring the remains. Near the principal cabins, I saw two bodies entire, with the exception that the abdomens had been cut open and the entrails extracted. Their flesh had been either wasted by famine or evaporated by exposure to the dry atmosphere, and they presented the appearance of mummies. Strewn around the cabins were dislocated and broken skulls (in some instances sawed asunder with care, for the purpose of extracting the brains), human skeletons, in short, in every variety of mutilation. A more revolting and appalling spectacle I never witnessed. The remains were, by an order of General Kearney, collected and buried under the superintendence of Major Swords. They were interred in a pit which had been dug in the center of one of the cabins for a cache. These melancholy duties to the dead being performed, the cabins, by order of Major Swords, were fired, and with everything surrounding them connected with this horrid and melancholy tragedy, were consumed. The body of George Donner was found at his camp about eight or ten miles distant, wrapped in a sheet. He was buried by a party of men detailed for that purpose."

To carefully lay out her husband's body, and tenderly to enfold it in a winding sheet, was the last act of devotion to her husband which was performed by Tamsen Donner.

With varying incidents and episodes, the immigrants all reached Sutter's Fort. One very attractive young lady received a proposal of marriage while doing her best to manage the rebellious mule on which she was riding. The would be lover pleaded his case well, considering the adverse circumstances, but the young lady gave not her consent.

Twenty-six, and possibly twenty-eight, out of the forty-eight survivors, are living to-day. Noah James is believed to be alive, and John Baptiste was living only a short time since at Tomales Bay,

California.   Besides these two, there are twenty-six whose residences
are known.   William McCutchen, who came from Jackson County,
Missouri, is hale and strong, and is a highly respected resident
of San Jose, California.   Mr. McCutchen is a native of Nashville,
Tennessee, was about thirty years old at the time of the disaster,
and has a clear, correct recollection of all which transpired.   Lewis
Keseberg's history has been pretty fully outlined in his statement.
He resides in Brighton, Sacramento County, California.

In May, 1847, Mary A. Graves married Edward Pile.   He was
murdered by a Spaniard in 1848, and this Spaniard was the first per-
son hanged in California under the laws of the United States.   In
1851 or 1852, Mrs. Pile married J. T. Clarke.   Their children are :
Robert F., born in 1852, who is married and living at White River,
Tulare County, Cal. ; Mattie, born in 1854, and now the wife of P.
Bequette, Jr., of Visalia ; James Thomas, born in 1857; an infant
who died soon after birth ; Belle, born in 1860, and died in 1871 ;
Alexander R., born in 1865, and Daniel M., born in 1872.   Mrs.
M. A. Clarke's address is White River, Tulare County, California.

Eleanor Graves married William McDonnell about the first of
September, 1849.   Their children are: Ann, born September, 1850 ;
Charles, born in 1852 ; Mary, born in 1855, married to Lester Green
January 2d, 1878, and now living on the Sacramento River about
seventeen miles below the city ; Lillie, born April 14th, 1857, died
in February, 1873; Franklin, born in 1860, died in March, 1873;
Henry, born July, 1864 ; Eleanor, born July, 1868 ; Leslie, born
October, 1872, died March, 1873; Louisa, born in 1878.   Mrs.
Eleanor McDonnell and family reside in Knights Valley, Sonoma
County.   Their address is Calistoga, California.

Lovina Graves married John Cyrus, June 5th, 1856.   Their children are : Henry E., born April 12th, 1859; James W., born February 16th, 1861 ; Mary A., born April 26th, 1863 ; Sarah Grace,
born December 11th, 1866 ; and Rachel E., born January 27th,
1873.   Their address is Calistoga.

Nancy Graves married Rev. R. W. Williamson in 1855.   Their
eldest, George, is an artist in Virginia City ; Emily is teaching school

in Knights Valley; Kate, Frederick, and Lydia Pearl are residing with their parents at Los Gatos, Santa Clara County, Cal.

William C. Graves is a blacksmith, living at Calistoga. He visited Truckee this Spring, examined the sites of the different cabins, and has rendered most valuable assistance in the preparation of this history.

The Murphys have always been well and favorably known in the best society of California. Mrs. Harriet F. Pike was married at Sutter's Fort in 1847, by Alcalde Sinclair, to M. C. Nye. Prior to the discovery of gold, they lived about three miles above Marysville, which, at this time, bore the name of Nye's Ranch. Mrs. Nye died in 1872 at Dalles, Oregon, and her remains were brought to Marysville and laid in the City Cemetery. Naomi L. Pike was married in 1865, to Dr. Mitchell of Marysville, moved to Oregon, became a widow, and is now the wife of John L. Schenck. Her address is, The Dalles, Wasco County, Oregon.

Mary M. Murphy was married in 1848, to C. Covillaud, then of Nye's Ranch, Cal. In 1850 the City of Marysville was laid out, and was named in honor of Mrs. Mary Covillaud. After lives of distinguished honor, Mr. and Mrs. Covillaud died, but there are now living five of their children. Mary Ellen is married to a prominent stock dealer, of Dalles, Oregon ; Charles J., a very bright and promising young man, is in the law office of his uncle, William G. Murphy ; William P., Frank M. and Naomi S., are all living at Dalles, Oregon. William G. Murphy resided at Marysville until 1849, when he went East to receive an education. He graduated with high honors at the State University of Missouri. He was married in Tennessee, returned to the Pacific Coast in 1858, and in 1863 was duly admitted a member of the bar of the Supreme Court of Nevada. He resided and practiced his profession at Virginia City until in the Fall of 1866, when he returned to Marysville, Cal. He now holds the position of City Attorney, and has an excellent and remunerative practice. He has a beautiful and charming home, and his family consists of him-

12

self, his wife and seven children. His eldest, Lulie T., was born in the Territory of Nevada, and his second child, Kate Nye, was born in Nevada subsequent to its admission as a State. William G., Jr., Charles Mitchell, Ernest, Harriet F. and Leander B., were born in Marysville.

Simon P. Murphy went back to Tennessee and married at his old home. He served in the Union army. He died in 1873, leaving a wife and five children.

William M. Foster gave his name to Foster's Bar, on the Yuba River. He died in 1874, of cancer. Of the children of Mr. and Mrs. Foster, there are now living, Alice, born in 1848; Georgia, born in 1850; Will, born in 1852; Minnie, born in 1855; and Hattie, born in 1858. Mrs. S. A. C. Foster has been residing in San Francisco, but her present address is, care of her brother, Wm. G. Murphy, Marysville.

Mr. and Mrs. Reed settled with their family in San Jose, California. Mrs. Margaret Reed died on the 25th of November, 1861, and her husband, James F. Reed, on the 24th of July, 1874. They are buried side by side, their coffins touching. Thomas K. Reed and James F. Reed, Jr., reside in San Jose, Cal. The latter was married March 16th, 1879, to Sarah Adams. Virginia E. Reed was married on the 26th of January, 1850, to J. M. Murphy. Their children's names are Mary M., born in 1850; Lloyd M., born in 1853; Mattie H., born in 1856; John M., born in 1858; Virginia B., born in 1860; J. Ada, born in 1866; Don James, born in 1867; Annie Mabel, born in 1871, and T. Stanley, born in 1874. Lloyd, Mattie and Mabel are sleeping in Oak Hill Cemetery, at San Jose, Cal. Mary was married to P. McAran, June 28th, 1869. Mr. McAran is one of the Directors of the Hibernia Bank and resides in San Francisco. Martha J. (Patty) Reed was married at Santa Cruz, Cal., December 25th, 1856, to Mr. Frank Lewis. They had eight children : Kate, born October 6th, 1857; Margaret B., born June 6th, 1860; Frank, born March 22d, 1862; Mattie J., born April 6th, 1864; James Frazier, born August 31st, 1866; a babe born May 30th, 1868, who died in infancy; Carrie E., born September 15th, 1870; and Susan

A., born December 31st, 1873.   Mr. Lewis died June 18th, 1876. Mrs. Lewis and her children reside at San Jose.

The family of Patrick Breen settled in 1848 at South San Juan, now in San Benito County, California.   Mr. Breen died December 21st, 1868, and Mrs. Breen April 13th, 1874.   John Breen was married in 1852.   His family are all living, and consist of his wife and ten children, whose names are: Lillie M., Edward P., John J., Thomas F., Adelaide A., Kate, Isabelle, Gertrude, Charlotte, and Ellen A. Breen.   Edward J. Breen was married in 1858, and his wife died in 1862.   His children are: Eugene, Edward, and Roger. Patrick Breen, Jr., married in 1865.   His wife is living, and their children's names are: Mary, William, Peter, and Eugene.   Simon P. Breen married in 1867.   His children are Geneva and Mary. James F. Breen married in 1870.   His only surviving child is named Margaret.   Peter Breen died, unmarried, in 1870, by accidental death.   Isabella M. Breen was married in 1869 to Thomas McMahon, and resides with her husband at Hollister, San Benito County, Cal.   Her brothers all reside at or near South San Juan, in the same county.

CHAPTER XXI.

NUSUAL interest attaches to the three little orphan children mentioned in a preceding chapter. Frances, Georgia and Eliza Donner, reached Sutter's Fort in April, 1847. Here they met their two elder sisters, who, in charge of the first relief party, had arrived at the Fort a few weeks earlier. The three little girls were pitiable-looking objects as they gathered around the blazing fire, answering and asking questions respecting what had taken place since they parted with their sisters at their mountain cabins.

Among the first to stretch forth a helping hand to clothe the needy children, was that noble philanthropist, Capt. John A. Sutter. Other newly-found friends gave them food from their scanty supplies, and the children would have been comfortable for a little while, had not some pilfering hand taken all that had been given them. They were again obliged to ask for food of those whom they thought would give. As the weather became warmer, it had a cheering influence over them, and they forgot their wish for heavier clothing; but oftener repeated the more heartfelt one—"If mother would only come!"

Only those who have suffered bereavement under similar circumstances can understand how fully these little girls realized their situation, when they were told that their mother was dead.

Not long after it became known that their parents were dead, Georgia and Eliza enlisted the sympathies of a kind-hearted Swiss couple, Christian and Mary Brunner, who lived a short distance from the Fort. Mrs. Brunner brought them bread, butter, eggs, and cheese, with the kind remark to those in whose hands she placed the articles, "These are for the little girls who called me grandma; but don't give them too much at a time." A few days later, upon inquiring of them how they liked what she brought, grandma was told they had not had anything, and was so surprised that she decided to take Georgia home with her for a week. Georgia was more delicate than her younger sister. Eliza was promised that she should be treated as kindly upon Georgia's return. The week passed, and Georgia returned, looking stronger. She told such wonderful stories about the many cows! lots of chickens! two sheep that would not let her pass unless she carried a big stick in sight! about the kindness grandma, grandpa, and Jacob, his brother, had shown to her, that it seemed to Eliza that the time would never come when she and grandma were to start to that enchanting home! Such a week of pleasure! Who but that little girl could describe it! Grandma's bread and milk gave strength to her limbs and color to her cheeks. She chased the chickens, and drove the cows; she brought chips for grandma, rode the horse for Jacob, and sat upon grandpa's knee so cheerfully, that they began to feel as if she belonged to them. But her week had come to an end! Grandma, all dressed for a walk to the Fort, sought the little girl, who was busy at play, and said, "Come, Eliza, I hear that Georgia is sick, and I am going to take you back, and bring her in your place." The sweet little girl looked very grave for a moment, then glancing up with her large black eyes into that dear old face, she took courage, and asked, with the earnestness of an anxious child, "Grandma, can't you keep both of us?"

This simple question provided a home for both until after Hiram

Miller was appointed their guardian.   He was entrusted with their money, obtained from Keseberg and from other sources.   The little sisters were then again separated.   Frances had found a home in Mrs. Reed's family.   Georgia was to go with grandpa, who was about to remove to Sonoma.   Eliza went to her eldest sister, who was now married and living on the Cosumnes River.   Here she remained until Winter.   Then hearing that Mr. Brunner's family and Georgia desired her return, she became so homesick that her sister consented to her going to them.   Fortunately, they heard of two families who were to move to Sonoma in a very short time, and Eliza was placed in their charge.   This journey was marked with many incidents which seemed marvelous to her child-mind.   The one which impressed itself most forcibly, occurred upon their arrival at the bank of the Sonoma River.   She was told that Jacob would meet her here and take her to grandma's, and was delighted that her journey was so near over.   Imagine her disappointment at finding the recent rains had raised the river until a torrent flowed between her and her anxious friends.   For days Jacob sought the slowly decreasing flood and called across the rushing stream to cheer the eager child.   Finally, an Indian, who understood Jacob's wish, offered to carry her safely over for a silver dollar.   Never did silver look brighter than that which Jacob held between his fingers, above his head, that sunny morning, to satisfy the Indian that his price would be paid when he and his charge reached the other bank.

What a picture this scene presents to the mind!   There is the Indian leading his gray pony to the river's side!   He examines him carefully, and puts the blanket on more securely!   He waits for the approaching child.   How small she is—not five years old!   How she trembles with dread as the swift current meets her eye!   Yet she is anxious to go.   One pleading look in the Indian's face, and she is ready.   He mounts; she is placed behind him; her little arms are stretched tightly around his dusky form!   He presses his elbows to his sides to make her more secure, and by signs warns her against loosening her grasp, or she, like the passing branches, will be the water's prey!   They enter the stream.   Oh! how cold the water is!

They reach the middle; her grasp is tighter, and she holds her breath with fear, for they are drifting with the current past where Jacob stands! But joy comes at last. They have crossed the river. There stands the pony shaking the water from his sides. The Indian takes his dollar with a grunt of satisfaction, and Jacob catches up the little girl, mounts his horse and hurries off to grandpa's, where grandma, Leanna and Georgia are waiting to give her a warm welcome.

Months passed pleasantly, but gradually changes began to occur. The war with Mexico ended, and gold had been discovered. All the men who were able to go, hurried off to the mines to make a fortune. The little girls gave up their plays, for grandma was not able to do all the work, and grandpa and Jacob were away. They spent seven years with Mr. and Mrs. Brunner. They were kindly treated, but their education was neglected. In 1854, their eldest sister, Elitha, and her husband, came to Sonoma, offered them a home and an opportunity of attending school. This kind offer was accepted. For six years Eliza remained in Sacramento, in the family of her sister Elitha. To her she was indebted for the opportunity she enjoyed of attending, for one year, with her sisters Frances and Georgia, St. Catherine's Academy, at Benicia, and the public schools of Sacramento.

Elitha C. Donner married Perry McCoon, who was subsequently killed by a runaway horse. On the 8th of December, 1853, Mrs. McCoon was married to Benj. W. Wilder. They reside on the Cosumnes River, a few miles from Elk Grove, Sacramento County, Cal., and have six children. Leanna C. Donner was married September 26th, 1852, to John App. They now reside in Jamestown, Tuolumne County, Cal., and their family consists of Rebecca E., born February 9th, 1854; John Q., born January 19th, 1864; and Lucy E., born August 12th, 1868, who reside with their parents.

Frances E. Donner was married November 24th, 1858, to William R. Wilder, and now resides at Point of Timber, Contra Costa County, Cal. Their children are: Harriet, born August 24th, 1859; James William, born May 30th, 1863; Frances Lillian, born July 17th, 1867; Asaph, born May 7th, 1870; and Susan Tamsen, born September 3d, 1878.   Georgia A. Donner was married November 4th, 1863, to W. A. Babcock.   Their family consists of Henry A., born August 23d, 1864 ; Frank B., born June 29th, 1866 ; and Edith M., born August 24th, 1868.   Their address is Mountain View, Santa Clara County, Cal.

Eliza P. Donner, on the 10th of October, 1861, was married to Sherman O. Houghton.   Mr. Houghton was born in New York City, April 10th, 1828, served in the Mexican war, was Mayor of San Jose in 1855 and 1856, represented California in the 42d and 43d Congress, and is at present a prominent member of the San Jose bar. Mr. and Mrs. Houghton have six children.   The youngest living was born in Washington, D. C., at which city his family resided during the four years he served as member of Congress.   Their children are : Eliza P., Sherman O., Clara H., Charles D., Francis J., and Stanley W.   Their youngest born, Herbert S., died March, 18th, 1878, aged 20 months.   Mary M. Donner, daughter of Jacob Donner, was adopted into the family of Mr. James F. Reed, in 1848.   She continued a member of this family until her marriage with Hon. S. O. Houghton, of San Jose, August 23d, 1859.   June 21st, 1860, Mrs. Mary M. Houghton died, leaving an infant daughter, Mary M., who is now a lovely young lady, and a member of the family of Mr. and Mrs. Houghton.

A short time after the arrival of George and Mary Donner in Yerba Buena, a number of the citizens contributed a fund to enter for each of them a town lot.   These lots were then being distributed among the residents of the town.   Upon the petition of James F. Reed, a grant was made to George Donner of one hundred vara lot number thirty-nine, and the adjoining lot number thirty-eight was granted to Mary.   The price of each lot was thirty-two dollars, and both were paid for out of the fund.   The grants were both entered of record by the Alcalde, George Hyde.   The grant made to George was signed by the Alcalde, but that made to Mary was through inadvertence, not signed.   A successor of Hyde, as Alcalde, regranted the lot of Mary Donner to one Ward, who discovered the omission of the Alcalde's name to her grant.   According to law, this omission caused her to lose her title. In 1851 a number of persons squatted on the lot of George Donner, and in 1854, brought suit against him in the United States Circuit Court, to grant them title. This suit was subsequently abandoned under the belief that George was dead. In 1856, a suit was instituted by George Donner, though his guardian, to recover possession of the lot. The result was a long course of litigation, which was not terminated until after George's death. The case was twice appealed to the Supreme Court of the State, and twice to the Supreme Court of the United States. Pending the litigation, George Donner sold his interest, for which he received a considerable sum of money.

THE END.